# HELPING CHILDREN TO TELL
# ABOUT SEXUAL ABUSE

# HELPING CHILDREN TO TELL ABOUT SEXUAL ABUSE

## Guidance for Helpers

ROSALEEN MCELVANEY

Jessica Kingsley *Publishers*
London and Philadelphia

First published in 2016
by Jessica Kingsley Publishers
73 Collier Street
London N1 9BE, UK
and
400 Market Street, Suite 400
Philadelphia, PA 19106, USA

*www.jkp.com*

**Library of Congress Cataloging in Publication Data**
Names: Mitchell, Gary (Gary George Ernest), 1985- editor.
Title: Doll therapy in dementia care / [edited by] Gary Mitchell.
Description: London ; Philadelphia : Jessica Kingsley Publishers, 2016. |
   Includes bibliographical references and index.
Identifiers: LCCN 2016005892 | ISBN 9781849055703 (alk. paper)
Subjects: LCSH: Dementia--Treatment. | Dolls--Therapeutic use. |
   Dementia--Patients--Rehabilitation.
Classification: LCC RC521 .D65 2016 | DDC 616.89/1653--dc23 LC record
available at http://lccn.loc.gov/2016005892

**British Library Cataloguing in Publication Data**
A CIP catalogue record for this book is available from the British Library

ISBN 978 1 84905 712 7
eISBN 978 1 78450 235 5

Printed and bound in the United States

# CONTENTS

# ACKNOWLEDGEMENTS

I'd like to thank those who shared this journey with me and brought this book to birth. Stephen Jones of Jessica Kingsley Publishers who encouraged me to submit my proposal, and followed through with persistence; a little encouragement goes a long way. To the many children, young people and adults, both clients and fellow professionals, with whom I have worked over the years and who have taught me so much; who have shared their pain and their joy; and whose words and experiences offer hope as well as understanding. I'd like to thank my 'readers', those who read an earlier draft of the book and gave so generously of their time and feedback: Patricia Clerkin, Katie Creighton, Niamh de Rossa, Siobhan McCarthy and Ann McCourt. To the team at Jessica Kingsley Publishers for being so easy to work with, including Danielle and Alexandra. To my wider family and friends who kept faith in me and whose belief in me spurred me on. To Gisella Stapleton for agreeing to grace the cover of this book with her beautiful painting. To my husband, Frank, for feeding me and trying (in vain) to keep me from overdoing it; and to my sons, Lorcan and Fergus, for putting up with me.

CHAPTER 1

# Introduction

Child protection is everyone's responsibility. Those of us who work with children have an added responsibility: to be there for children when they need to tell us if someone is hurting them. Child sexual abuse typically occurs in secret. We know from research that this secret is sometimes never divulged and for most it can remain hidden for many years. As a society, if we don't know about this problem, which transcends age, gender, socioeconomic and cultural barriers, we are constrained in our ability to address it. We need to know about it in order to stop it, thus preventing further harm to the child; we need to know as other children may be at risk from a particular perpetrator. We need to be able to reach out and help. The child may need professional support to address the psychological impact of the abuse. The perpetrator needs assistance in order not to do this again.

Professional helpers are well placed to help children disclose – they have access to information and resources and can thus educate themselves about sexual abuse; they have the advantage of spending time with children outside the family home, and so can be very well placed to notice when something is wrong; they have a mandate to draw attention to a child when they are distressed or 'out of sorts'; and in many countries they have a statutory obligation to report a concern about sexual abuse. But, most of all, those who work with children *care*. It is from this caring standpoint that helpers are well placed to act upon their concerns to ensure that a child gets the help that is needed.

Helpers are understandably anxious about dealing with the issue of sexual abuse. It is an emotive topic. People have strong views about it and are very quick to judge if we make a mistake and 'get it wrong', whether that be in the way we talk with children or in our actions in response to concerns that a child is being abused. We know that we can inadvertently influence children's views about their world, so we have to be careful in our conversations in order to give children an opportunity to talk and not to ask inappropriate questions that can confuse them further. In an effort to protect ourselves from criticism from others, we can be reluctant to engage children in conversations that may open up something that we feel unable to deal with. Talking about these anxieties is important: having someone to go to when we are uncertain about how to deal with the situation and knowing where to get help when we need it will help us feel more competent and able to respond to children in ways that help them rather than harm them.

In the past 20 years, many countries have developed *child abuse awareness campaigns* in an effort to raise awareness about the nature of sexual abuse, the extent of it and the importance of recognizing the possibility of abuse early in the cycle of abuse. Such campaigns may include child abuse prevention programmes, delivered in schools, with the aim of educating children about abuse and equipping them with the social skills to tell someone if something like this is happening to them. It is difficult to evaluate prevention programmes. How can we tell if something has worked when its aim is to prevent something from happening? How do we know whether it would have happened or not, regardless of the intervention? And when we are trying to prevent something that is so hidden in society, how do we know that we have been successful in preventing abuse or simply that children are not talking about it? What we do know from evaluations of such programmes is that they are effective in educating children about abuse: children demonstrate a better awareness of abuse and what to do if something happens to them following such programmes.[1] School-based awareness programmes have been found to provide a safe environment in which to promote disclosure.[2] I know from my own clinical experience that many children approach teachers

---

1   Lalor and McElvaney (2010). A full reference list in alphabetical order is available at the end of the book.
2   Barron and Topping (2010).

following such programmes and disclose experiences that they have previously told no one about. Nevertheless, the extent to which these children can transfer learning and assertiveness skills into real-life situations and actually prevent abuse from occurring is still unknown.

One of the criticisms of such prevention programmes is the burden they place on children to disclose abuse. It is the responsibility of adults to protect children. When we think of a five-year-old girl, it seems unfair that we expect her to be the one to raise the alarm. When we add to this the difficulties that children and adults have in disclosing experiences of sexual abuse and the help they need in order to do so, it doesn't just seem unfair – it seems unconscionable. Such programmes were never designed to be the sole focus in preventing child abuse, but the lack of commitment of resources has meant that in many countries they are the only prevention measure used. Every two years the International Society for the Prevention of Child Abuse and Neglect publishes a review, *World Perspectives*, which examines child protection measures globally. It is interesting to see the differences between countries in terms of child abuse prevention efforts. This is not necessarily related to economic resources. Policies and legislation in an individual country can be seen to reflect how seriously the issue of sexual abuse is regarded: whether there are laws requiring citizens to report concerns of child abuse and neglect, state-sponsored child protection programmes in schools, therapeutic support services for children and families where abuse is a concern, statutory obligations to investigate concerns of child abuse and neglect, and therapeutic support services for offenders. All of these measures represent to some extent how much a society cares about its children.

Over the past 20 years, research on *child sexual abuse disclosures* and clinical practice with children and adults who have experienced sexual abuse has improved our understanding of the dynamics of sexual abuse and in particular the dynamics of disclosing such experiences. We now know a lot more about the extent to which children do not tell about abuse experiences and we have a substantial body of research that helps us understand the reasons for this. While earlier research tended to be of a survey nature, based on large samples, in more recent years we have a solid body of work that has involved interviewing those who have had these experiences. This gives us a more in-depth awareness of the complexities involved in disclosing sexual abuse. This research has highlighted the need to focus our prevention efforts, not so much on the child developing the skills to tell but on the potential recipients of disclosure – parents, community workers, teachers and friends – and their ability to hear.[3] *The research has emphasized the importance for children of having someone to tell whom they can trust, of having an opportunity to tell that doesn't rely exclusively on them approaching an adult and of receiving an appropriate response when they do begin to tell.*

## Why write a book for helpers?

It is better for children if they tell sooner rather than later. If we can help children tell early on, there is a greater likelihood that the abuse can be stopped. However, the benefits of prompt disclosure extend beyond this. In addition to reducing the likelihood of re-occurrence, prompt disclosure also reduces the likelihood of further victimization and psychological difficulties. A 2004 study found that children who had experienced more psychological distress symptoms were more likely to delay disclosing their experiences (delay is defined as more than one month from the onset of the abuse). Telling an adult was most helpful if this happened within 30 days of the onset of the abuse.[4]

As professional helpers, we are well placed to notice when children are in need of help. The opportunity for the child to tell often comes about because someone recognizes the child's cues and probes further. In order to help children tell, caregivers need to initiate conversations with children, be prepared to listen to them and follow up on the cues that they offer.[5]

Young people may tell a professional before they tell anyone else, but professional helpers are not typically the first port of call for

---

3    Allnock and Miller (2013); Collin-Vézina *et al.* (2015); Cossar *et al.* (2013); Jensen *et al.* (2005); McElvaney, Greene and Hogan (2014); Staller and Nelson-Gardell (2005); Ungar *et al.* (2009a); Ungar *et al.* (2009b).
4    Kogan (2004).
5    Jensen *et al.* (2005).

children disclosing sexual abuse.[6] However, in a study in South Africa, 52 per cent of children first told someone outside the family – someone from the community (32%), a policeman (12%) or a teacher (8%).[7] The researchers found that the stimulus for disclosure was more likely to be detection by another rather than purposeful disclosure by the child and argue for the active engagement of members of the wider community in working together to prevent sexual abuse.

Jeanette Cossar and her colleagues in the United Kingdom[8] examined an online discussion forum that young people engaged with for the purpose of the study. In marked contrast to previous research, professionals were identified as the group that young people most often told, followed by friends and family. Responses to the posts often recommended that the young person should tell someone: professionals (suggested 160 times), family (suggested 60 times) and friends (suggested 36 times). Teachers and youth workers were identified as being particularly helpful as people to tell, along with social workers as people to go to for help.

## Learning from research on young people's negative experiences with professionals

When the Council of Europe was preparing its campaign and developing its strategy for prevention of violence against children, they consulted with children and young people about their experiences of engaging with professional services.[9] The young people they spoke with described being cautious about public services, not knowing where to go to for help and how to access help, feeling frustration at not being listened to when they did have an opportunity to speak, and not being heard or believed and taken seriously. Young people said they wanted their contact with professionals to be based on mutual trust and respect.

---

6   Vincent and Daniel (2004); Priebe and Svedin (2008).
7   Collings, Griffiths and Kumalo (2005).
8   Cossar *et al.* (2013).
9   Council of Europe (2012).

A study in the United Kingdom[10] examined why young people felt they were not believed by professionals when they reported abuse and/or neglect. Four key issues emerged: 1) young people felt they and their family were treated as a problem or as troublesome; 2) they felt that professionals made up their own mind about whether the allegation was true, which could deter young people from disclosing further; 3) they felt judged by professionals about how they dressed or behaved; and 4) they described a reluctance on the part of professionals to believe them if the alleged perpetrator was a respected member of the community or held a position of authority.

Similar themes were identified in a study in Australia.[11] Children and young people talked about professionals not listening to them and not believing them. They also spoke of professionals not being well informed and not being able to listen to the children's very difficult experiences.

## How helpers can help

Young people say that the three things they want most from professionals are that they should give an effective response, be knowledgeable and be available.

Research on *effective professional responses* highlights the importance of the personal qualities of professional helpers.[12] Young people have talked about trusting individuals rather than agencies, highlighting aspects of professional relationships that were felt to promote trust. These include duration of the relationship, being believed, not being judged and closeness. Offering effective support entails providing accessible and available services. Young people also want professionals to be reliable, to respect privacy, to stay engaged with the young person and to take action to change the situation.

*Awareness of sexual abuse* is both a requisite for recognizing that the abuse is occurring and for being able to disclose abuse early on in the abuse process. Recognition that abuse is occurring often starts with an emotional awareness that things are not right before

---

10  Tucker (2011).
11  Mudaly and Goddard (2006).
12  Cossar *et al.* (2013).

the child is able to identify the problem themselves, never mind be able to communicate it to others.[13] Although research shows that young people weigh up the pros and cons of telling, there is also an emotional battle going on – what I refer to in my work as the 'pressure cooker effect'.[14] Young people often come to the attention of services, not through what they say but through their behaviour, thus highlighting the importance of professionals noticing children's distress and not expecting them to be able to verbally describe what is going on for them. When professionals respond sensitively and show concern for a child, the child can open up and talk.

*Facilitating awareness* is helping the young person to become aware of their rights, to know what is right and what is wrong, to be able to recognize abuse when it is happening and to know where the responsibility lies when someone abuses a child. As many abusers are adept in techniques of grooming children into abusive interactions, it can be difficult for children to recognize when this is happening. Teaching them about their rights and building their skills in knowing when something is wrong can help them along the pathway of telling. Part of awareness is understanding. For many children it is difficult to understand what is happening when they are being abused. This impacts on their ability to recognize the behaviour as abusive. By facilitating awareness in children, we also facilitate understanding, by helping them make sense of what is happening to them.

What information do young people need? Some of the questions that young people have are in relation to identifying whether behaviour is abuse or not, what to do if they are being abused, whether to tell or not, who to tell and how to access help.[15]

*Facilitating expression* focuses on how we can help to create conversations with children that provide the opportunity for them to tell. Even when professionals are not the first recipient of a disclosure, we do play a significant role for children who do not have a parent to turn to, perhaps because the parent is struggling with their own difficulties, relationships with parents are poor,

---

13 Cossar *et al.* (2013).
14 McElvaney, Greene and Hogan (2012).
15 Cossar *et al.* (2013).

the parent is the perpetrator or young people are concerned about how their parents will react. Studies of young people and factors promoting positive mental health point to the importance of young people having one good adult they can turn to for support.[16] This adult may be a teacher, a sports coach, a youth worker, a counsellor, a community volunteer, a member of the police force, or anyone who works with children and young people in a caring capacity.

Young people have described how conversations about their distress helped them to recognize for themselves that they were experiencing abuse. They also found that relationships of trust helped them to tell.

*Taking action* on the information we receive from children can help to make their lives better. Containing the secret of sexual abuse is a burden to children. When we act on information children give us, we help to alleviate that burden. In taking action, it is important to include children as much as possible in decision-making processes – to respect the need for young people to maintain some control over the process when they tell. In the Council of Europe consultation, young people identified their right to participation in decisions affecting their lives as the one that is respected the least, noting their experience of exclusion from civil life and important decisions that affect their lives. They identified barriers to their meaningful participation as age limits on the right to be heard, low levels of information, adults' prejudice and lack of listening skills, intimidating formal settings, and tight timeframes. The fear of loss of control over decisions is one of the reasons identified by some researchers as preventing young people from telling.[17]

## Overview of this book

Below, I provide a brief outline of each chapter. I introduce a format that will be followed in Chapters 4, 5, 6 and 7, that is, the use of three headings to frame each of these chapters: 'What the research says', 'Minding myself' and 'How to help'. 'Key messages' are offered

16  Dooley and Fitzgerald (2012).
17  Cossar *et al.* (2013).

at the end of every chapter. I suggest that the three key ways we use to help children and young people are facilitating awareness, facilitating expression and facilitating action. It is important that we learn from research conducted in this field and that we use that research to inform how we interact with children in dealing with this very sensitive topic. However, it is equally important that we reflect on our own belief systems and feelings about such a highly emotive topic. Child sexual abuse evokes multiple and complex emotional reactions in all of us. These reactions can both help us and hinder us in our role as helper. If we can approach this subject area with both a scientific mindframe (research informed) and be mindful of our own personal position (person informed) we can be better able to be present for children in ways that put them at the centre of the conversations and ensure that their needs are met. Improving our own awareness helps us to support this capacity in the children we work with. Thus, there is an emphasis throughout the book on the importance of self-awareness and support for helpers in having conversations about sexual abuse with children.

*Chapter 1* has, I hope, given the reader an overview of why I think it is so important for us as helpers to facilitate children along the pathway of disclosure. In drawing on both my clinical experience and research of children's experiences, I highlight particular themes in this book. My hope is that the following chapters will give a good enough overview of the field to help helpers feel confident with their own knowledge about the issue.

*Chapter 2* provides an overview of the current state of knowledge on child sexual abuse and its prevalence, including definitions of sexual abuse in different jurisdictions and information about who is perpetrating this abuse. The chapter will also give an overview of what we know about the psychological impact of child sexual abuse and how it impacts on children in different ways.

*Chapter 3* summarizes key research on what we know about children's experiences of disclosing child sexual abuse, the extent to which children delay in disclosing such experiences, the conceptual models that have been developed to help us understand the disclosure process and the factors that have been identified as either helping or hindering children in disclosing sexual abuse.

*Chapter 4* highlights a key theme that has emerged from our research with children and young people – the importance of believing children. Despite the growing awareness of sexual abuse, children continue to be afraid that if they tell someone they have been abused, they will not be believed. Adults continue to doubt children when they disclose.

*Chapter 5* focuses on non-verbal indicators that something is not right in the child's world. Information on how children may present following experiences of sexual abuse will be given to inform the reader as to what signs to look out for, taking care not to over-interpret or jump to conclusions. The section on 'Minding myself' addresses how our own experiences (or lack of experiences) can lead us to misinterpret children's behaviours and what we need to do to make sure that this does not get in the way of how we talk with children about these behaviours.

*Chapter 6* provides a rationale for the importance of asking children questions in order to provide them with the opportunity to tell. Guidance is offered for helpers in how to create these opportunities, and how to mind yourself in this context.

*Chapter 7* examines children's experiences of blaming themselves for the abuse and how shame and self-blame can prevent them from telling. The possible psychological impact on the helper of listening to children's stories of sexual abuse is also discussed. Helpers need to be careful not to exacerbate children's distress and find ways to alleviate children's negative experiences.

*Chapter 8* presents the evidence on peer-to-peer disclosure and discusses how helpers can support young people in how they respond to their friends when sharing confidences that need to be brought to adults' attention. How these peers respond to such disclosures is crucial for the psychological wellbeing of both the young person who discloses and the young person to whom the disclosure is made. This chapter addresses how we as helpers can both facilitate this adaptive behaviour and at the same time support young people through the process to ensure that they get the help they need.

*Chapter 9* discusses research on children's experiences following disclosure and highlights the types of support that children need following such disclosure. Supporting children is complex and challenging, particularly when helpers themselves may feel disheartened and frustrated with the wider systemic response to the child's disclosure.

# CHAPTER 2

# Child Sexual Abuse and Its Impact

This chapter will provide an overview of child sexual abuse – how it is defined, its prevalence and the psychological impact of child sexual abuse.

## Defining child sexual abuse

In the absence of evidence to the contrary, it is safe to assume that the sexual abuse of children has always been a feature of human interactions. Kevin Lalor in *The End of Innocence*[1] refers to literature describing sexual offences against children as early as the 1400s and an alarmingly high proportion of allegations of rape or attempted rape of children (over 9000) in France in the late 1800s. The phenomenon appears to disregard cultural, socioeconomic, gender and age boundaries. As Finkelhor[2] notes, 'in every locale where it has been sought, researchers have demonstrated its existence'.

The national guidelines in Ireland, Children First: National Guidance for the Protection and Welfare of Children,[3] specifically outline the range of behaviours that constitute sexual abuse. They refer to behaviour whereby a child is used by another for the purpose of sexual gratification. This behaviour may include exposing a child to either sexual organs or intentional sexual activity in front of a child;

---

1   Lalor (2001).
2   Finkelhor (1994), p.412.
3   Department of Children and Youth Affairs (2011), p.9.

touching a child for the purpose of sexual arousal; masturbation that is either carried out in the presence of the child or where it directly involves the child; penetrative sexual intercourse – oral, anal or vaginal; showing sexually explicit material to a child; recording a child being engaged in sexual activity; or manipulating images of children for sexual purposes.

This definition is a broad definition, attempting to encompass both contact and non-contact abuse. It can be difficult for people to understand and appreciate the violation involved in exposing children to sexually explicit behaviour or material and the traumatic impact this can have on children's developing selves. The definition does not include female genital mutilation (FGM), which is also considered to be a form of sexual abuse.[4] The World Health Organisation defines FGM as a procedure that intentionally alters or causes injury to the female genital organs for non-medical reasons, is mostly carried out on girls between infancy and 15 years of age and is a violation of girls' human rights.[5]

The definition does not specify an age cut-off point, rather using the term 'child'. From a legal point of view, the definition of a child and the age of consent varies from country to country. The definition rather focuses on the behaviour evident in child sexual abuse: the child being used by another for gratification or sexual arousal. By doing so, it draws attention to the violation of the child's rights.

## The challenges of determining prevalence rates of child sexual abuse

While some countries, particularly those in the Western hemisphere, have been more prolific in their research on this topic, it is now recognized that child sexual abuse is a global phenomenon. When we look at the studies on prevalence, we see differences between

---

4 There is an extensive body of research on child sexual exploitation that is beyond the scope of this book (see Melrose and Pearce 2013 and www. gov.uk/government/uploads/system/uploads/attachment_data/file/278849/ Safeguarding_Children_and_Young_People_from_Sexual_Exploitation. pdf).
5 www.who.int

these rates, not necessarily because there are real differences in how prevalent sexual abuse is in different cultures but because of the way information was gathered, who it was gathered from and how sexual abuse was defined in these studies (for example, some studies only include contact abuse, while others include non-contact abuse as well). We know that prevalence rates for penetrative abuse are lower than other forms of abuse. The legal age of consent also varies from country to country, making true comparisons difficult. What is legally child sexual abuse in one jurisdiction is not child sexual abuse in another.

When we look at 'clinical samples', that is, samples of children or adults who attend therapeutic or medical services, we find a much higher proportion of individuals with a history of sexual abuse. However, this excludes children and adults who may have been abused but did not seek professional help. Similarly, if we look at 'legal samples', we only learn about individuals who make a formal complaint to the police. Samples of young people in state care or who are homeless show a disproportionately high prevalence of children who have experienced sexual abuse.[6]

The most reliable studies are what we call 'national probability studies'. In such studies, a lot of effort is put into selecting a representative sample of a population, that is, with different socioeconomic cohorts, children of different ages and children from different family constellations. Random sampling is used in such studies so that every individual in a population has an equal chance of being included in the sample. These studies therefore have the ability to capture a sample that can give us information about the population in that country. If, for instance, 15 per cent of such a sample report that they have experienced child sexual abuse, we can say with confidence that 15 per cent of the general population are likely to have experienced child sexual abuse. Even in these studies, however, we find that many people do not respond to surveys. When my colleague Kevin Lalor and I carried out a review of international prevalence studies, we found that in large-scale studies in Ireland, the United States and Sweden (of adults), and in

6   Lalor and McElvaney (2010).

China (of high-school students), approximately 30 per cent did not respond.[7] We do not know whether this 30 per cent were more likely to be people who had been abused and did not want to participate in the survey because they did not want to reveal it, or people who had not been abused and therefore saw the survey as not relevant to them, or people who simply did not have the time to take the call or complete the questionnaire, or people who did not respond for other reasons unrelated to the nature of the study.

There has been some debate about the reliability of surveys in terms of whether people are prepared to disclose experiences of sexual abuse, given the difficulties in disclosing that are well documented and will be discussed in detail in Chapter 3. However, most studies in the past ten years have included an interesting question: how many people had never disclosed prior to the survey? One survey after another is revealing significant percentages of individuals – both adolescents and adults – who have never told anyone prior to the survey. Some argue that people are less likely to reveal experiences of sexual abuse to a stranger, yet these surveys suggest the contrary – significant proportions of respondents disclose sexual abuse for the first time in these surveys. Perhaps, in fact, it is easier to tell a stranger on the telephone than to confide in someone within one's own family or social network. This suggests that far from the prevalence studies being an underestimatation of the prevalence of child sexual abuse, these studies may more accurately reflect the real prevalence of the issue.

Some authors have criticized the practice of relying on self-reports in estimating prevalence rates in populations of children and young people. However, if such studies confined themselves to samples where the abuse had been 'proven' in legal proceedings, they would omit the significant proportions of sexual abuse reports that never find their way into the court systems. As Cross and colleagues[8] point out, '[m]ost substantiated and founded child abuse cases do not lead to prosecution and instead are the sole province of child protective services'.

---

7   Lalor and McElvaney (2010).
8   Cross *et al.* (2003), p.333.

# Prevalence of child sexual abuse across the globe

When Kevin Lalor and I reviewed the published prevalence studies in 2010, we found significant variation depending on who the researchers sampled (community samples vs. clinical samples), and how they defined sexual abuse (penetrative abuse vs. contact abuse vs. non-contact abuse). Nevertheless, we found that most studies *reported prevalence rates of sexual abuse for boys at below 10 per cent and between 10 per cent and 20 per cent for girls.*

Table 2.1 summarizes the findings from authors who have reviewed a number of studies, bringing together the information to give us a global view of child sexual abuse prevalence.

Table 2.1 Prevalence of sexual abuse across the globe

| Author | No. of studies or countries | Rate for men | Rate for women |
|---|---|---|---|
| Finkelhor (1994) | 19 countries | 3–29% | 7–36% |
| Lampe (2002) | 24 countries | 1–15% | 6–36% |
| Stoltenborgh et al. (2011) | 217 studies | 6.6–8.8% | 6.4–19.7% |

Studies that have used meta-analysis, that is, an additional analysis of data already gathered in other studies, have been able to compare the prevalence of sexual abuse across continents and compare studies that rely on informants (parents or professionals) with those that rely on self-report. A meta-analysis of 65 child sexual abuse prevalence studies from 22 countries worldwide[9] showed that the highest prevalence rates were in Africa (Morocco, Tanzania, South Africa) at 34.4 per cent and the lowest were in Europe (Portugal, United Kingdom and Spain). Another meta-analysis of 217 studies published between 1982 and 2008[10] (total sample of nearly 10 million, across the globe) showed an estimated prevalence rate that was 30 times higher than the estimate suggested from informant studies (that is, where reports were made by professionals).

---

9   Pereda *et al.* (2009).
10  Stoltenborgh *et al.* (2011).

Where countries have the benefit of having conducted large-scale studies at two points in time, it is possible to see whether there has been a change in the prevalence rate of sexual abuse. Some such studies suggest that there has been a decline in the prevalence of sexual abuse over the past 20 years.[11]

We know from these large-scale studies that:

- more girls are abused than boys

- penetrative abuse is more infrequent than other 'contact' abuse

- most children are abused by someone they know

- only a tiny proportion of children are abused by 'strangers'

- while babies can be sexually abused, most children are in the middle childhood years when they are abused.

However, these studies have not captured the prevalence of online sexual exploitation. While the internet has opened up a range of opportunities for children, it has also introduced newer ways of accessing vulnerable children and presented challenges for young people in navigating their way through this new medium in a manner that protects them from exploitation. In the European Union Kids Online study, drawing on information from countries across Europe, 15 per cent of young people aged 11–16 had received sexual messages or images from their peers.[12] Studies from Sweden have documented significant percentages of girls and boys posting sexual images and videos online and these being circulated against their will.[13] Table 2.2 summarizes information from a few large-scale studies specifically examining young people's exposure to sexually explicit material on the internet, such as nudity and sexual activity.

---

11  Radford *et al.* (2011).
12  Livingstone *et al.* (2011).
13  Ungdomsstyrelsen (2009).

Table 2.2 Prevalence of exposure to sexually explicit material on the internet

| Author | Sample | Rate for boys | Rate for girls |
|---|---|---|---|
| Bra (2007) | 7500 (14–15-year-olds) | 18% | 48% |
| Bulijan Flander et al. (2009) | 2880 (10–16-year-olds) | 36% | 15% |

Another study[14] highlighted the prevalence of young people (21% of young people aged 12–16 years) who had experienced someone talking with them about sex over the internet. More than a third of these conversations were with strangers. Much of this sexual contact, though, is through peer-to-peer messaging.

Young people are increasingly meeting new people online, which results in offline contact, some of which is sexually abusive. In a Norwegian study,[15] 35 per cent of the boys and 26 per cent of the girls stated that they had met someone face to face who initially was an online contact. Less than 5 per cent of these meetings had led to sexual harassment or abuse. A study of young people's use of chat rooms on the internet[16] found that 28 per cent (35% of girls and 23% of boys) reported having been asked inappropriate questions about sexual experience, private body parts, clothes and experience of masturbation, and there had been suggestions about meeting up or engaging in sexual activity. One study[17] described 129 sexual offences against juvenile victims (13–15 years) who met an adult offender through internet chat rooms. Most of the young people had sex with the adult on more than one occasion. In one Swedish study,[18] 58 young girls were groomed and lured into a sexual relationship with a man who pretended to be a woman online.

14  Medierådet (2010).
15  Suseg et al. (2009), cited in Quayle, Jonsson and Lööf (2012).
16  Buljan Flander, Cosic and Profaca (2009).
17  Wolak, Finkelhor and Mitchell (2004).
18  Wagner (2008), cited in Quayle et al. (2012).

Despite a decline in the prevalence of female genital mutilation over the past three decades, a report by UNICEF[19] in 2016 notes that over 200 million girls and women alive today have been cut in this way and if current trends continue, it is likely to increase in coming decades. FGM is rarely if ever noted in studies on child sexual abuse.

Finally, with increased mobility across the globe, the trafficking of children and the sexual abuse of unaccompanied asylum-seeking minors has become a major problem that is not captured in large-scale prevalence studies. The literature refers to significant numbers of children being trafficked from Albania to European countries – 4000 between 1992 and 2002.[20] A UNICEF report[21] described children being trafficked to Denmark, Finland, Iceland, Norway and Sweden and experiencing sexual exploitation (prostitution and pornography). In the United Kingdom, studies note the sexual abuse in England of unaccompanied asylum-seeking minors from Ethiopia, Eritrea and Somalia.

# The intergenerational nature of child sexual abuse

We know from clinical experience that a large number of children who experience sexual abuse come from families where at least one parent (and in some cases both) has been sexually abused. I vividly recall Anne (not her real name), a young mother who was horrified to discover that her child was being abused by her father – she left her child with her parents while she went out to work. One might ask: How could she do this? Leave her daughter with the very person who abused her? What did she expect? The truth is that it never occurred to her that her daughter was at risk. Although she had been for counselling herself, the matter had never been reported to child

19 UNICEF (2016) *Female Genital Mutilation/Cutting: A Global Concern.* Available at www.unicef.org/media/files/FGMC_2016_brochure_final_ UNICEF_SPREAD.pdf, accessed on 15 April 2016.
20 Gjermenia *et al.* (2008).
21 UNICEF (2011).

protection authorities and no investigation had taken place as to whether he presented a risk to other children. Her own experience of abuse had taken place many years beforehand. She didn't know anything about paedophilia, about the addictive nature of sexually abusive behaviour. She thought it was just her – that there was something about her that contributed to his abusing her. She didn't see – couldn't see – that her daughter might be at risk. Nevertheless, when her daughter began to show signs of distress and saying disjointed things about her grandfather and her 'pee pee', she did act on the information and contacted a social worker. She was open about her own experiences of abuse and open to the possibility that her father had abused her child, even though this would then lead to the realization that if she had said something about her father, her own daughter might have been spared this experience.

It is likely that Anne, like many others, managed to cope with the aftermath of the abuse experience by putting it out of her mind, moving on with her life and in many ways 'forgetting all about it', an everyday coping mechanism that we all have of not wanting to think about something, so we put it away in our minds. Anne was able to leave her daughter with her parents, knowing her father would be alone with her from time to time, but this did not raise alarm bells for her because she had 'forgotten all about' her own experience of abuse. She did not see a connection between then and now, between herself and her daughter. It is not that she ran through an argument in her head – she did not convince herself consciously, as some people do, that there was nothing to worry about, that the abuse happened years ago and now things were different, that it was in her past and here was her darling beautiful daughter whom no one could want to hurt. She didn't even think about it. She was oblivious to the risk. It is unfortunate that she did not get some help with this when she went for counselling. It is one of the arguments for mandatory reporting, as those who have been abused can be very poor judges of whether someone is a risk to other children.

# Psychological impact of child sexual abuse
## Frameworks for assessing psychological impact

As sexual abuse encompasses a broad range of behaviours, in many different kinds of relationships, and varying from a one-off or a few incidents to ongoing abuse over a number of years, the psychological impact varies. Children can experience low self-esteem, difficulties such as anxiety, depression, anger and aggression, substance abuse, somatic difficulties, self-harming behaviour, dissociation and sexual difficulties.[22] The impact of sexual abuse extends beyond psychological distress – this distress in turn impacts on social and physical health problems to a much higher extent in the longer term than is found in those who have not been sexually abused.[23]

John Briere[24] provides a useful framework for how we might understand the psychological impact of a traumatic event, by thinking about *the nature of the event, the characteristics of the individual, the individual's response to the event* and *the response of others.* How well or how poorly a child copes with the impact of the abuse can depend on these four variables. In applying this to the sexual abuse experience, the 'event' itself may have more impact if it is at the more severe end of the spectrum of abusive behaviours (penetrative abuse), if it is accompanied by physical violence or if the child experienced ongoing abuse over an extended period of time. Characteristics of the individual refer to the child's own personal resources such as personality, temperament and capacity for regulating their emotions. These will influence the individual response to the sexual abuse experience, but this is also influenced by how the child makes sense of the experience. I am reminded of a young person whose individual response to being abused was disgust, dismissing it as an example of 'crazy behaviour' and clearly the responsibility of the abuser. She shrugged it off and did not appear to be upset by the incident. Another young girl of about the same age had a similar experience. However, she was shocked and horrified and experienced an overwhelming feeling of shame as

---

22 Briere and Elliott (2003).
23 Dube *et al.* (2005).
24 Briere (1997).

to why the abuser had 'picked' her. Finally, the response of others is evident in how supportive parents, carers and other significant people in the child's life are following disclosure. A range of studies have shown that children whose parents or carers respond to the disclosure in a believing, supportive manner have better longer-term mental health outcomes.[25]

In the case of interpersonal trauma, such as when a child is sexually abused, the relationship between the child and the abuser is a significant factor in considering the psychological impact. While it is a crucial factor in determining whether and when the child discloses such abuse, it also makes the process of overcoming the psychological impact of the abuse experience much more complicated as children struggle with competing loyalties, conflicting emotions and the significant betrayal of trust inherent in such trauma.

Suzanne Sgroi and her colleagues, Porter and Blick, first described what they called the *'damaged goods syndrome'* in their book *Handbook of Clinical Intervention in Child Sexual Abuse*.[26] This idea captures the experience of the child that something is wrong with them as a result of having been abused. The child internalizes the badness and feels bad as a result of being involved in the 'bad' experience. According to these authors, children may feel *guilty*, either as a result of being explicitly told by the abuser that it was their fault or through implicit messages where nothing is said by the abuser but the child feels that they should have stopped the abuse. In addition to feeling responsible for the abuse, many children feel responsible for the aftermath of the disclosure. In many cases, there is no 'trouble' until the child told. The child therefore feels that they are the cause of all the trouble. Unfortunately, this belief is reinforced by others in the child's network and children may actually be blamed for causing disruption by disclosing. As one young person I interviewed described it: '[I] should have kept it to myself.' Children may experience *fear* – a fear of the abuser or a fear that the abuse will happen again. Many children are threatened by the abuser that something terrible will happen if they do not comply with the abuse

---

25  Lovett (2004); Ullman (2007); O'Leary, Coohey and Easton (2010); Easton (2012).
26  Sgroi, Blick and Porter (1982).

or if they tell. This may manifest as anxious behaviour, and it may take the form of *sleep difficulties* – difficulty getting to sleep, waking up in the night, difficulty getting back to sleep and nightmares. Children may experience *depression* and appear withdrawn and/or sad. This may manifest in *psychosomatic symptoms* such as tummy pains or headaches and children may appear to suffer from a lot of physical illnesses. They may suffer from *low self-esteem* and *poor social skills* as a result of the psychological impact of the experience. They may experience *repressed anger* and *hostility* towards the abuser or towards others close to them. They may have an *impaired ability to trust* due to the breach of trust experienced in the abuse situation. They may struggle with *blurred role boundaries* and *role confusion*, putting the needs of others, such as their parents, before their own, or feeling like an adult due to being involved in sexual behaviour. This can result in a *pseudomaturity*, feeling 'grown up' in a 'sexual relationship' where they feel special, or feeling responsible for protecting younger siblings from the abuser. Finally, children can experience difficulties with *self-mastery* and *control* as they try to cope with the overwhelming emotions associated with the abuse experience and struggle to keep these emotions in check.

Another framework that has been widely used was developed by David Finkelhor and Angela Browne.[27] This has been used by professionals in assessing the psychological impact of child sexual abuse and in suggesting how to support children with specific areas of difficulty. They described four dynamics that they saw as unique to the experience of sexual abuse, as distinct from other forms of childhood abuse or neglect. The four dynamics are *traumatic sexualization, stigmatization, betrayal and powerlessness*.

1. *Traumatic sexualization* describes how the child is engaged in sexual activity that is inappropriate to the child's developmental level. The child may learn to associate sexual 'favours' with special attention, which is often craved or enjoyed by the child, thus leading to confusion in loving and caring relationships. The child may experience a level of sexual arousal as a result of the sexual contact, leading

---

27 Finkelhor and Browne (1985).

to sexual preoccupation, compulsive masturbation or acting out sexually with other children. As the child gets older, the normal developmental questions over sexual identity experienced in adolescence can become fraught with negativity, particularly if the child was abused by someone of the same gender.

2. *Stigmatization* refers to the guilt and shame that so many children feel as a result of being abused. This can stem from explicit verbal messages they received from the abuser that the abuse was their fault or it can result from the child's own feelings about the abuse feeling bad and this being internalized as somehow being their fault (similar to the 'damaged goods syndrome' described above). The child may be coerced into participating actively in the sexual behaviour, resulting in them feeling complicit in the abuse and therefore sharing responsibility for it. When the child keeps the secret, this exacerbates the feeling of self-blame, which in turn isolates the child from peers and family. The child may feel very different to others and like 'damaged goods', resulting in difficulties with self-esteem and guilt.

3. *Betrayal* is always a feature of child sexual abuse. For the most part, children are sexually abused by someone they know. Children typically view adults or those older than them as people to be trusted, people who look after them. When a child is abused, this trust is manipulated and betrayed. Children lose their core belief that the world is a safe place and their expectations that they will be protected and cared for. This loss can be devastating for children and can manifest itself through attachment difficulties where children can become either clingy to caregivers and insecure in their absence or distrustful of others, hostile and aggressive. The experience of betrayal often results in the loss of a child's ability to judge who can be trusted and who can not, resulting in trusting others too easily or not trusting at all.

4. *Powerlessness* is a dynamic that captures a feature of all child abuse: the imbalance of power that is such a key feature of the abusive relationship where the child is violated by someone more powerful – physically or emotionally. The loss of the child's ability to prevent or stop the abuse undermines their sense of self-efficacy and autonomy, which is so crucial to their development and sense of identity. Fear is often a feature of the abuse experience, and repeated experiences of fearfulness result in difficulties such as nightmares, anxiety/phobias, depression and somatic complaints. The child may internalize this powerlessness, manifested in nightmares, anxiety/phobias, depression and somatic complaints or may externalize the powerlessness, manifested in aggressive behaviour, bullying or engagement in criminal activity.

These dynamics help us to understand why children who have experienced sexual abuse develop difficulties such as depression, anxiety, eating disorders and substance abuse.

# Risks for further sexual exploitation or revictimization

Experiencing sexual abuse in childhood is a significant risk factor for later sexual revictimization.[28] Children who experience sexual abuse in childhood are at greater risk of being abused in adolescence and in turn at even greater risk of being abused in adulthood. We know this from studies of adults, dating back to Diane Russell,[29] who found that almost twice as many women who experienced sexual abuse by someone within the family before the age of 14 experienced rape or attempted rape after the age of 14. This finding has been replicated in other studies in other countries (Ireland, Sweden, New Zealand and South Africa) relying on adult samples.[30] One study[31] found

---

28  Classen, Palesh and Aggarwal (2005); Lalor and McElvaney (2010).
29  Russell (1986).
30  See McElvaney and Lalor (2014) for review.
31  Humphrey and White (2000).

that the risk was up to 13 times higher for those who experienced rape or attempted rape during adolescence. This has been found in both retrospective studies – asking adults about their childhood experiences – and prospective studies – where young people are interviewed and then followed up and asked about experiences many years later.

Another area of risk for those who have experienced child sexual abuse is that of engaging in high-risk sexual behaviour: early onset of consensual sexual activity in women, teenage pregnancy, having more than five sexual partners before the age of 18, having multiple partners, group sex, unprotected sexual intercourse and sexually transmitted diseases.[32] Studies of prostitution and sex workers have found a disproportionately high history of penetrative childhood sexual abuse in both women and men. This is evident both in large-scale studies of people drawn from the general population and from studies of prostitutes and sex workers. The risk of high-risk sexual behaviour is greater if the sexual abuse was penetrative and also if the abuse was by a family member.

One might think that this can be explained by the family and home environment, attachment history or substance abuse in the home. However, studies have provided controls for these and have still found statistically significant findings pointing to the link between childhood sexual abuse (penetrative) and later high-risk sexual behaviours. Several possible explanations have been offered:

- Leaving home at a young age leaves young people vulnerable to victimization.

- It is possible that due to the impact of the abuse children seek emotional gratification in unhealthy relationships.

- Young people may seek out high-risk situations to achieve a specific emotional state (such as getting a 'high') or may be unable to recognize high-risk situations as a result of avoidant coping strategies.

---

32  See McElvaney and Lalor (2014) for review.

- Feelings of hopelessness and despair may leave young people at risk of seeking short-term pleasures and ignoring long-term impact.[33]

- Young people themselves attribute their decision to become involved in prostitution to their experience of sexual abuse.[34]

## Many children do not experience negative psychological impacts

Not all children suffer negative psychological consequences from the experience of sexual abuse. One study[35] of adolescents in the United States, using a range of measures looking at post-traumatic stress disorder, depression and substance abuse in the year previous to the survey, found that 45 per cent of the young people who had experienced sexual abuse reported no symptoms of distress. It can be argued that the long-term impact of sexual abuse does not become evident until individuals are older. Many adults have reported doing fine until some event or experience in adulthood triggers a range of conflictual feelings about their childhood experiences.[36] However, a longitudinal study in the Isle of Wight[37] that followed up men and women from childhood until their mid-40s found that of those who disclosed experiences of physical or sexual abuse in childhood (approximately 10% of the sample), about 45 per cent reported no negative psychological symptoms arising from these experiences in their adult lives. The authors of the report attributed this to protective factors such as parental care, positive peer relationships during adolescence, individual personality and the quality of adult relationships.

Some adults who have experienced sexual abuse in childhood (and other kinds of traumatic experiences) have described positive outcomes from these experiences, sometimes referred to in the

---

33 Slonim-Nemo and Mukaka (2007).
34 Silbert (1982); Bagley and Young (1987).
35 Kogan (2004).
36 McElvaney (2002).
37 Collishaw et al. (2007).

literature as 'post-traumatic growth'.[38] This may be in the form of a greater appreciation or sense of gratitude for life, a sense of greater personal strength or resilience and a better understanding of themselves and their relationships with others.[39] According to Scott Easton,[40] people typically describe this growth in three areas: 1) their view of themselves (as stronger, more resilient, more compassionate towards themselves); 2) their life philosophy (sense of meaning of life or spirituality, gratitude for what they have, greater appreciation of their lives and the impact of this on life priorities); and 3) relationships with others (empathy, altruism and feeling closer to others). He found that men's understanding of the abuse was related to higher levels of growth. By understanding, he meant being able to place the responsibility for the abuse on the abuser, understanding their own response to the experience of the abuse and the responses of their parents or caregivers, and understanding how the experience of abuse had impacted on them in terms of their emotions and their behaviour.

Psychological research has confirmed clinicians' experience that in order to resolve much of the psychological impact of traumatic experiences, it is necessary to confront the experience, to think about it, to bring it out into the open as it were, to face up to it, talk about it and allow the intense emotions associated with the experience to surface. It is through this opening up that the issues can be talked about, felt and resolved. For many, the primary coping strategy used to deal with the impact of the abuse is to not allow these feelings to surface. The child may fear that they will lose control of themselves. Many adults in therapy speak about the fear of 'losing it' and 'going mad'. While this strategy is adaptive in the shorter term – it allows the child to manage themselves and to get on with the daily-living tasks that face them, such as going to school, mixing with friends and getting by – it becomes maladaptive over time. Avoiding feelings associated with the abuse can develop into avoiding feelings about anything that is potentially

38  Tedeschi and Calhoun (2004).
39  Lev-Wiesel, Amir and Besser (2005); see Helgeson, Reynolds and Tomich (2006) and Linley and Joseph (2004) for reviews.
40  Easton et al. (2013).

upsetting – or pleasurable and exciting. The child narrows their repertoire of emotional experiencing in order to protect themselves from the unpleasant emotions that surface when they think about the abuse. This then impacts on other parts of their lives – their peer relationships, their relationships with family members – and over time, their intimate relationships as young and older adults.

## Key messages

- Child sexual abuse is a global phenomenon affecting at least one in ten boys and up to one in five girls.

- Sexually abusive behaviours can range from penetrative abuse to contact abuse to non-contact abuse.

- Psychological impact varies according to the individual child and how others respond to them.

- Children may experience a range of long-term difficulties and may need significant support in order to address these difficulties.

- Being sexually abused can leave children vulnerable to later exploitation.

- It is difficult to predict how an experience impacts on a child. It is important not to assume that a particular type of abuse will impact on a child more negatively than another type of abuse.

- Not all children experience psychological difficulties as a result of being sexually abused.

- Thinking about the experience, talking about it and allowing the feelings associated with the experience to surface, helps.

# CHAPTER 3

# Containing the Secret

## What We Know About Child Sexual Abuse Disclosure

This chapter will give an overview of the research to date on what we know about children's experiences of disclosing child sexual abuse, the extent to which children delay in disclosing such experiences, who they tell and, to some extent, what influences children in telling or not telling. I will draw extensively on the qualitative studies that have been carried out in the past 15 years that have enhanced our understanding of this complex and challenging process. This field of study is still growing. Various authors, including myself, have developed theoretical frameworks to help us understand the disclosure process for children and adults. We have not reached a consensus as yet, but there are common themes to the frameworks that have been proposed and these will become clear to the reader in this chapter.

We know from studies of adults that most individuals who experienced sexual abuse in childhood did not tell until adulthood. It is only in the past two decades that research studies have been designed to specifically examine children's experiences of disclosure. Earlier studies captured some information about these experiences but were not specifically focused on the disclosure experience. Nevertheless, one of the distinguishing features of these study findings was that most children did not tell immediately when they were abused.

The research studies in this area have used a range of methods to gather information about children's experiences of disclosing sexual abuse. Large-scale population surveys, designed to gather information about the prevalence of sexual abuse, have also included questions about disclosure – for example, who the child disclosed to. Smaller-scale studies have gathered information from children and families who attend services or who have engaged with the legal system. Sometimes this entails interviewing children and sometimes the information is extracted from children's files. On the basis of this research and clinical literature, we have known for many years about the extent to which children delay disclosing and we have known something about the reasons for these delays. Through qualitative or interview studies that focus specifically on children's experiences of disclosure, we have arrived at a better understanding of how complex the process of disclosure is and how each individual has their own unique experience of this process.

There are limitations with every study. Studies with adults rely on recall of experiences many years before. As we develop, we reflect on our experiences, trying to make sense of them. This impacts on our perception of these experiences and the 'accuracy' of our recall of the actual experience. Our memories of experiences change with the passage of time. Reflection on experiences brings different understandings, both of how people experience events and how they perceive the way others responded to them. We feel differently about experiences when we have had the time to reflect on them or talk with others. However, there are also strengths in retrospective studies. These can capture multiple stories of disclosure over an extended period of time, and they may offer a fuller picture of the process and how it unfolds over the lifespan. They may also include individuals who may not have presented to services for help and who may not have told anyone about their experiences prior to a survey. Such studies may then be more representative of the entire population of those who have experienced abuse than what we learn from studies of children or adults who present to services. Studies with children and adolescents, one can argue, may be more reliable as the experience of abuse was more recent. However, these young people may not have a good understanding of what influenced their experiences in telling. It is sometimes with the benefit of reflection that we come to understand what influences us in our choices and decisions in life.

## Delays in telling

Children for the most part, do not tell immediately. We know from studies of adults who were abused in childhood that most never told as a child. Kamala London and colleagues reviewed a range of studies and found that between 55 per cent and 69 per cent of adults did not disclose as children.[1] Between 70 and 75 per cent of survey respondents said they delayed five years or more (or never told).[2] The most important factor that influences this delay is the relationship between the child and the abuser. This is true across all types of studies – population surveys, clinical samples or criminal samples.[3] The sexual abuse and violence in Ireland (SAVI) study in Ireland[4] involved interviews with over 3000 adults, and 47 per cent of those who said they had such an experience, said that this was the first time they told anyone. A study of adolescents in the United States[5] found that only 14 per cent told within 24 hours of the incident; 26 per cent of their sample of young people had not told an adult of their experience of abuse prior to the survey.

Even when children do come to the attention of the authorities, many deny that abuse occurred, despite medical evidence to the contrary[6] or videotaped evidence of the abuse.[7] Children do recant allegations of abuse (that is, take them back) when they have in fact been abused. The extent to which this happens is unknown but it appears to be evident in a small number of children. Children are more likely to recant allegations when the abuser is someone close to them.[8] It also appears to be more a feature of younger children's experiences. Although this affects a small number of children, the psychological fallout from such an experience is complex and has a significant impact on the child's relationships with important people in their lives.

1   London *et al.* (2007).
2   Smith *et al.* (2000); Hébert *et al.* (2009).
3   Lyon and Dente (2012); see McElvaney (2015a) for review.
4   McGee *et al.* (2002).
5   Kogan (2004).
6   Lyon (2007).
7   Sjöberg and Lindblad (2002).
8   Goodman-Brown *et al.* (2003); Hershkowitz, Lanes and Lamb (2007); Malloy, Lyon and Quas (2007).

Reporting sexual abuse to the authorities is even more uncommon. When discussing 'disclosure' we need to distinguish between 'informal disclosure' and 'formal disclosure'. Informal disclosure I refer to as *confiding*. A confidence is shared, usually with a trusted other. Formal disclosure when referred to in the literature usually refers to a disclosure to a professional – a formal reporting of the matter to the authorities, be that civil (child protection) or criminal (police). The studies above refer to informal disclosure. Studies of formal disclosure in adults and children show much lower rates. One study of adult men in the United States found that 15 per cent reported to the authorities,[9] while a study of adolescents in Norway[10] found that only 8.3 per cent had talked to professionals about the abuse.

## Who children tell

Studies that rely on clinical samples of children alone tend to suggest that most children tell their parents first. It is only when we ask children directly about their disclosure experiences that the full picture emerges with regard to who children tell. Studies of young people have found that fewer than half of the children told parents first.[11] Younger children tend to confide in a parent or trusted adult, while older children have more of a tendency to confide in peers before telling adults.[12] In a study of adolescents in Norway,[13] of those who had disclosed their experience of abuse, 42.6 per cent of the boys and 37.9 per cent of the girls mentioned 'friend of my own age' as the only person they had told.

---

9  Easton (2012).
10 Priebe and Svedin (2008).
11 Collings *et al.* (2005); Hershkowitz *et al.* (2007); McElvaney *et al.* (2012).
12 Crisma *et al.* (2004); Hershkowitz, Lanes and Lamb (2007); Kogan (2004); London *et al.* (2007).
13 Priebe and Svedin (2008).

## How parents respond to disclosure of sexual abuse

Some of the research on how parents respond to their children's disclosure shows that although most mothers are supportive, they can be inconsistent and ambivalent towards their children as they struggle to come to terms with the reality that their child has been abused.[14] Studies have suggested that supporting parents leads to better adjustment for both parents and children; a strong response that conveys protection and support leads to better mental health and social functioning.[15] Children who are satisfied with the level of support they receive from parents are less depressed and experience higher self-esteem.[16] Ramona Alaggia and her colleagues[17] advocate peer support programmes for parents following disclosure to help them cope with their own reactions and help them support their children.

However, many children continue to experience negative reactions from caregivers following disclosure. In one study,[18] children who were abused by non-family members described feeling ashamed or afraid of parents' responses – and many of their parents did tend to blame their child or be angry towards them. This study found a strong relationship between what children expected and the actual reactions of their parents.

## Process of disclosure

Earlier research in this field saw disclosure as an event, a one-off occurrence, rather than a process that unfolds over time. Qualitative research that enabled a more in-depth examination of the child's experience, from their perspective, has firmly established that it is a process that not only unfolds over time the first time a child discloses, but continues across the lifespan as the child or adult continues to

---

14  Elliott and Carnes (2001).
15  Lovett (2004).
16  Rosenthal, Feiring and Taska (2003).
17  Alaggia, Michalski and Vine (1999).
18  Hershkowitz *et al.* (2007).

confide in others. Children tell in different ways. Based on her work with adult male and female survivors of childhood sexual abuse, Ramona Alaggia[19] suggested that *four categories* capture the range of disclosure experiences:

1. *Purposeful disclosure* describes direct and indirect verbal attempts and intentional behavioural attempts to disclose. The child or adult makes a conscious decision to tell and approaches another with the intention of telling. This appears to be the case for a minority of individuals. A child may tell in a purposeful manner, but it may be unplanned. Young people have described how, in the midst of an argument with their parent, they disclosed in anger. While it was intentional at the time, they did not plan to tell and in some cases may not even have wished to tell.

2. *Behavioural manifestations* include both intentional and non-intentional behavioural attempts to disclose or behavioural effects or symptoms. Children's distress can be seen as an attempt to communicate that all is not well in their world. They may not have the words to describe their experiences or may have difficulty articulating what has happened due to emotional distress. With younger children in particular, the telling may be prompted by an adult noticing unusual behaviour or comments made by the child, which are followed up and lead to a disclosure. For many teenagers, it is in the context of parents or others asking them about their psychological wellbeing that they have an opportunity to tell.

3. *Disclosures intentionally withheld* include intentional withholding, false denial, accidental discovery and prompted or elicited disclosure. For many children it is through the context of a conversation about themselves or about abuse in general that the opportunity may have presented itself and this prompted the young person to tell.

4. *Triggered disclosures of delayed memories* refers to the triggering of memories that may have been previously inaccessible.

19 Alaggia (2004).

Memories may be triggered by conversations about something that reminds the individual of the abuse; they can be prompted when the individual's children reach the age they were when they were abused; they can emerge when a person engages in counselling and begins to explore other childhood experiences.

The process of disclosure has been described by many as moving from more indirect communications such as distress, acting-out behaviour and risk-taking behaviour towards more direct strategies such as disclosing verbally to professionals.[20]

Many authors have helped us understand why it is that children keep the secret. The child, according to Roland Summit,[21] accommodates to the experience of abuse and *keeping the secret is seen as a way of coping with the experience*. Not talking about it helps the child manage the psychological impact of the abuse by avoiding the feelings that might emerge if they were to think about it or talk about it. Summit likened this process to that experienced by concentration camp inmates. Tilman Furniss,[22] a psychiatrist and family therapist, described the sexual abuse experience as a syndrome of secrecy, highlighting how the child uses secrecy as a way of adapting to the experience, a way of helping them manage the psychological and social impact of the experience.

The idea that children and young people need an *opportunity to tell* has been emphasized in recent studies. Karen Staller and Debra Nelson-Gardell describe the process of disclosure as a three-stage process: 1) the young person comes to terms with how they feel about the abuse and makes a decision to tell; 2) they seek out a trusted other and a time and place; 3) the consequences of telling in turn inform later experiences of telling or not telling, depending on the positive or negative consequences of their experience of disclosure. Children anticipate possible reactions of others, and how a person responds to the disclosure influences whether and how the child will disclose further or again to another person. Each experience

---

20  Ungar *et al.* (2009a, 2009b); Cossar *et al.* (2013).
21  Summit (1983).
22  Furniss (1991).

of disclosure impacts on subsequent decisions to tell. It is a lifelong process. Children and young people continue to evaluate trust and likely responses in new relationships. As one of Staller and Nelson Gardell's young girls said, 'it's never finished, never'.[23]

*Most children's disclosures are prompted rather than spontaneous.* Staller and Nelson-Gardell's process suggests that children make a decision to tell. However, more and more studies are indicating that most children disclose in response to an adult engaging with the child in conversation. Tine Jensen and her colleagues in Norway[24] suggest that disclosure is about a dialogue where children need to be provided with an opportunity to talk about sexual abuse and this needs to be prompted by an adult. Many disclosures result from someone recognizing the child's cues and asking questions as a result. One study[25] found that 43 per cent of their sample of 30 children only told after they were directly asked. Another study[26] noted that detection by another was found to be more likely to lead to disclosure than any purposeful disclosure on the part of the child. Jensen and her colleagues suggest that in encouraging disclosures caregivers need to be prepared and sensitive in initiating conversations or following up on non-verbal cues that the child offers. They also note that the child may need to be ready themselves before being able to engage in these conversations. This raises the question: how much help do children need in order to disclose their experiences of abuse and how can adults offer this help?

## Containing the secret

My own work has attempted to build on these earlier studies. Based on my interviews with children and young people, their parents and adults who experienced abuse in childhood, I developed a conceptual framework that sees disclosure as a process of *containing the secret*[27] (see Figure 3.1). This process involves three key dynamics, whereby children and young people: 1) *actively withhold* the secret; 2) are torn

---

23 Staller and Nelson-Gardell (2005), p.1426.
24 Jensen *et al.* (2005).
25 Hershkowitz *et al.* (2007).
26 Collings *et al.* (2005).
27 McElvaney (2008); McElvaney *et al.* (2012); McElvaney (2015b); Schönbrucher *et al.* (2012).

between needing to tell and wanting to keep the secret (*the pressure cooker effect*); and 3) *confide* in the context of a trusting relationship. The term 'containment' stems from what I see as the need for the child to contain the information about their experience. The clear conscious and active attempts on the part of the children and adults I interviewed to keep the secret, coupled with their increasing need to share the secret (the pressure cooker effect), spoke to me of a need to contain:

- their fears of what would happen if they told
- their fears of what would happen to them if they didn't tell
- their wish to seek support from others
- their wish to protect others from this terrible information
- their shame and fears of being judged by others
- their drive to shed this self-blame and put the responsibility where it belonged – with the abuser.

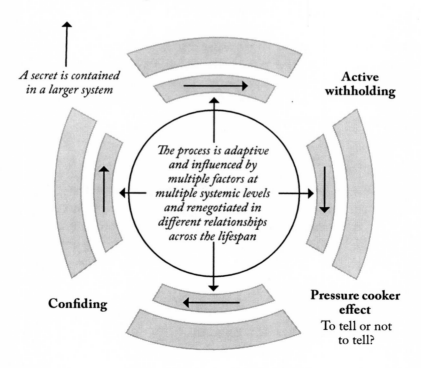

**Figure 3.1** Containing the secret of child sexual abuse

## 1. ACTIVE WITHHOLDING

Active withholding reflects the agency of the child or young person in not telling, stemming from a range of fears and concerns, such as not wanting people to know what had happened to them. Some of the young people were asked directly if they had been abused and they denied it; others were asked about their distress and they denied that anything was wrong. One boy's older sister came upon his older cousin behaving suspiciously with another child. She asked him had anything happened to him. He denied it vehemently. It was another seven or eight years later, after he had told his friends about the abuse, that he was able to tell his sister. Some made up stories to deflect attention away from themselves in their attempt to keep the secret. Some described wanting to tell someone, thinking about it, planning how they would do it, but having difficulty saying the words. According to one 16-year-old girl:

> I wanted to say something but I just couldn't... It was almost as if I was trying to speak but my voice was just cut off – it was like I was just miming it but nothing was coming out.[28]

Many said that it was easier not to tell than to tell. Some described how difficult it was to say the words. This doesn't just refer to the first time a child tries to tell. Some of the young people I interviewed described this difficulty in several contexts and relationships. Finally, the active withholding was evident in the attempt to keep the secret following disclosure. When they did tell someone, there was an ongoing need to contain the secret by trusting only a few people and by asking for confidentiality to be kept so that others would not know. Older children talked about not wanting certain friends to know out of fear that they would tell others. Parents talked about not wanting extended family members to know, amidst concerns that they would feel differently towards the child or concerns that there would be violent consequences for the abuser. This attempt to confine the secret also referred to young people's reluctance to share more details. Many described how they partially disclosed, waiting to evaluate the reactions to disclosure before being able to share

---

28 McElvaney *et al.* (2012), p.1163.

more details. At a broader systemic level, beyond the family, there was also an attempt to contain the secret insofar as in many cases the schools that the children attended were not aware of the abuse.

Actively withholding the secret, before anyone is told of it, may give the child a sense of having control over their own experience – a means of containing themselves in the midst of the chaos. Keeping the secret may be a way of taking control by managing the flow of information and the distress that is felt when sharing the information. By not talking about it, the child can protect themselves from the psychological distress that is felt when talking or thinking about the experience. This may be too overwhelming for the child to face and so containing the secret by actively withholding may be a way of not thinking about the experience and regulating the emotional impact of the abuse.

## 2. THE PRESSURE COOKER EFFECT

This process refers to the dilemma that the child faces in both wanting and not wanting to tell. Children described feeling psychologically distressed, sometimes making attempts to tell. For example, a young girl went into her mother's bedroom on more than one occasion and hid a note in her mother's bed, telling her about the abuse; then ran in and took the note back. Sometimes it was as if the young people reflected on the possible consequences when they swayed back and forth in their decision whether to tell or not. Some described how the emotional burden of not telling became too much – one 16-year-old boy described how he tried to bury it, but it kept coming back up to the surface. The pressure cooker effect captures the experience of pressure building up, both in keeping the secret and in wanting to tell. One 13-year-old boy said:

> I just felt bad really like holding it in... It was just like I had to tell or it was just gonna be there for ever and ever and it's just gonna annoy me. I just had to tell.[29]

---

29 McElvaney *et al.* (2012), p.1164.

Other young people described not being able to hold it in any longer. For many, the opportunity to tell was what 'blew the lid off the pressure cooker'. A family argument, a TV programme about abuse, constant questioning about their emotional state – these were described as triggers that prompted the young person to tell. Many of these disclosures were unplanned. Although the children and young people may have thought about telling and weighed up the pros and cons, the disclosure itself for many 'just happened'.

The idea of a pressure cooker captures the struggle between conflicting emotions. Arnon Bentovim and William Friedrichs, in writing about the emotional impact of sexual abuse on children, note the importance of a child's capacity for emotional self-regulation. Bentovim[30] describes the abused child's experience as 'overwhelming' and 'beyond control'. He talks about the inability of the child to process the experience, to think about it and make sense of it so that the child can assimilate this experience. Annie Rogers[31] refers to the trauma as 'the unsayable…something that moves toward speech and away from speech at the same time'. The pressure cooker effect then represents the building up of emotional pressure, contributed to by being asked questions about their wellbeing or their behaviour, competing with the wish to keep the secret. The unplanned nature of many disclosures fits with this idea.

## 3. CONFIDING

Telling about sexual abuse is not just telling about something that happened. It is an extremely private experience and for the most part was only told to someone who was trusted – a confidante. Thus, the experience of confiding was defined in terms of who was told (a trusted person) and the context of telling – a sharing of personal and private information and the wish for confidentiality as expressed by the young person – all of which emphasize the 'confiding' nature of the telling. For some young people, the context of confiding was in a peer group where there was a mutual sharing of confidences. The wish for confidentiality to be maintained was clearly articulated by young

---

30 Bentovim (1992).
31 Rogers (2006), p.57.

people in this study and reflected their fears about the consequences of telling and their need for this information to be contained. Young people spoke of fears of friends or even family members talking to others about the disclosure. The need for confidentiality both influenced young people's decisions to tell and continued to be felt after confiding in another.

Containing the secret is seen as an adaptive psychological response to the experience of abuse, a way of making this experience manageable, of coping with the anxiety associated with the experience of abuse. The child is an active agent in keeping the secret as a means of regulating what may feel like unmanageable emotions, thus protecting themselves and others from the reality of the abuse.

## What stops children telling and what helps children to tell?

The factors that influence keeping the secret are, as David Jones noted, 'multidetermined'[32] and may be unique for each child. There are a number of reasons why we cannot rely on children to come to us and spontaneously tell us that they have been abused. These may relate to age, gender, type of abuse, relationship to the abuser, and strategies used to enlist the child's compliance.[33]

There are mixed views as to whether it is easier or more difficult for younger children or older children to disclose sexual abuse. There are reasons why younger children may find it easier (they are more inclined to spontaneously disclose without understanding the possible consequences of telling) and also reasons why older children may find it easier (knowing that it is wrong and wanting to protect other children). There are reasons why younger children find it more difficult to tell (not having the language or understanding to describe what has happened and thinking it is a game) and older children delay more in telling (feeling ashamed or embarrassed about what happened and fearing the consequences of disclosing).

---

32 Jones (2000).
33 Paine and Hansen (2002).

Often children do not understand what has happened. They do often instinctively know that it is wrong and that it is something that should not be talked about, even if they have not been told to keep it a secret. While younger children may not have the language – the words – to tell us they have been abused, children also often have difficulty recognizing that what is happening is sexual abuse. Older children and teenagers often want to be self-reliant. They believe that they can cope with the situation themselves.

Older children are inclined to disclose more purposefully, that is, with intent, and they will give more detail about the experience. Younger (pre-school) children tend to be more vague in their descriptions and will typically disclose accidentally, without intent. Boys are more reluctant to disclose than girls, and children who have disabilities, be they cognitive, physical or emotional, tend to delay more in telling. Children who are concerned about their parents' emotional wellbeing tend to delay more in telling, particularly when they are older. Children who feel supported by their parents, particularly their mothers, are more likely to tell more promptly. Children abused by a family member are more likely to delay telling than children abused by a non-family member. Children who experience more severe forms of abuse (for example, penetration), and children who are abused over a longer period of time, delay more in telling than children who experience less physically intrusive forms of sexual abuse. Children who experience post-traumatic symptoms (avoidance, intrusive thoughts or images and hypersensitivity) are more likely to delay telling than children who have fewer symptoms. When the abuser has been aggressive and physically threatening the child, longer delays in telling are evident. However, when the abuser uses more coercive strategies, such as giving a child extra attention or treats, this has also been found to result in delays in the child telling. There is some evidence that children who participate in school-based child abuse prevention programmes will disclose following such programmes.

One study specifically looked at what predicts delays in disclosure.[34] Tina Goodman-Brown and her colleagues examined

---

34 Goodman-Brown *et al.* (2003).

US attorney files of children and found that the child's age (at the time of reporting), whether the abuse was intra-familial or extra-familial, whether the child felt responsible for the abuse or not, and the child's fear of negative consequences following disclosure determined the time to disclosure. Children who were older, were abused by someone within the family, who felt more responsible for the abuse and who feared negative consequences following disclosure took longer to tell. As was also highlighted by Tine Jensen and her colleagues in Norway, Goodman-Brown's work noted the importance of children's expectations about other people's reactions to and their tolerance for the disclosure as influencing children's decisions to tell.

This book draws on a number of studies relying on interviews with young people about their experiences of disclosing childhood abuse. Michael Ungar and colleagues in Canada interviewed adolescents about what they saw as barriers to disclosing experiences of violence (not just child sexual abuse). I interviewed children, teenagers, their parents and adults who experienced childhood sexual abuse in Ireland. Schaeffer and colleagues[35] examined 191 files of children who were seen for a sexual abuse evaluation in the United States. My colleague, Maebh Culhane, and I did a similar study, drawing on information from children's files about their experiences of disclosure.[36] Sharon Jackson and colleagues[37] analyzed 2986 cases of child sexual abuse in children aged 5–18 years from a children's helpline in Scotland. In the United Kingdom, Jeanette Cossar and colleagues[38] interviewed young people individually and in focus groups and examined an online forum for young people on the topic of sexual abuse. Verena Schonbrucher and colleagues interviewed 26 adolescents aged 15–18 in Switzerland.

Some of the key issues that emerge from these studies and ones that I will discuss in greater detail in this book are: the importance of *being believed*, having an opportunity to tell or *being asked*, having a sense of responsibility, *shame or self-blame*, and the importance

35  Schaeffer, Leventhal and Asnes (2011).
36  McElvaney and Culhane (2015).
37  Jackson, Newall and Backett-Milburn (2015).
38  Cossar *et al.* (2013).

of peer influence or *helping friends tell* and *what happens after first disclosure.*

In my own research, I found that the distinction between barriers to telling and facilitators is unhelpful, as what might be a barrier for one child could be a facilitator for another child or even for the same child. An example of this is 'concern for others'. Some children were prompted to tell out of a concern that other children might be at risk of being abused by the person who abused them. Many of these same children were concerned about how upset their parents would be if they found out – this acted as a barrier to them telling.

When we think about the factors that influence disclosure, it is helpful to use an *ecological lens*, drawing on the work of Jay Belsky and Uri Bronfenbrenner. The child and their experience of abuse and disclosure is seen in the context of their own development with their own individual risk and protective factors but also in the broader context of their family, peer network, local community and wider culture. The child brings their own psychological resources to dealing with the experience of abuse but is influenced by others in their family and social network and by the societal and cultural context in which they live. Both Ramona Alaggia and Delphine Collin-Vézina and their colleagues[39] have used an *ecological framework* in their studies of adults who experienced childhood abuse and I have used this lens to examine the various factors identified in my own research.[40]

Taking an ecological perspective helps us to take account of the factors noted above – shame, self-blame, the expectations of others (in particular, fears of being believed) and being provided with the opportunity to tell – and can impact on the child's ability to tell. This broader lens also helps us to understand the impact of context on the developing child. When a child is experiencing other forms of maltreatment within a family, it impacts on their ability to disclose sexual abuse. Other family dynamics are also important, such as communication patterns in families and rigid gender roles, sibling relationships and relationships in the extended family. Children's experiences of broader social contexts are also

39 Alaggia (2010); Collin-Vézina *et al.* (2015).
40 McElvaney (2015b).

important – particularly school and community supports. Also at a societal or sociocultural level, how children's voices are heard in society, the extent to which a country legislates for child protection, the social stigma and taboos about sexuality and sexual abuse, racism, and how media portrays children, sexuality and sexual abuse all act as both inhibiting and facilitating factors in influencing a child's disclosure. Collin-Vézina and colleagues[41] also highlighted the additional sociocultural barriers experienced by men who are abused by women and the social norms relating to men as victims, and confusion regarding sexual orientation experienced by boys and men who experience childhood abuse.

## Summary

The literature discussed above highlights how difficult it is for young people to tell, and the complexity of the factors influencing this process. It is clear that children actively keep the secret of sexual abuse, with large proportions of children not disclosing until adulthood. On the basis of the adult surveys described and the proportion of adults who first disclosed in the context of a survey, it is safe to assume that there are individuals who have never disclosed such experiences. Children weigh up the risks of telling. They will anticipate adults' reactions and they often get this right. Anticipated negative reactions from parents or caregivers will prevent them from telling. The 'pressure cooker effect' operates both as a barrier to telling and an impetus to tell. Even when young people want to tell and are ready to tell, it can be difficult to say the words. Disclosure is clearly a dialogue, a conversation between two people. Children rely on adults to initiate conversations with them in order to provide an opportunity to tell. Many children, particularly teenagers, will tell a friend before they tell an adult. Disclosure is a process – it takes place over time, in different contexts and to different people, and it continues across the lifespan. Each experience of disclosure will influence the next experience. Giving children enough good

---

41  Collin-Vézina *et al.* (2015).

experiences will help them disclose when they need to. Professional helpers who understand how difficult it is to talk about sexual abuse can respond sensitively to young people who may be on a pathway to disclosure.

## Key messages

- Children who have been sexually abused need containment to cope with the psychological impact of abuse. Keeping the secret is their way of containing themselves.

- Most children do not tell immediately. Many delay for several years, often into adulthood, and some never tell.

- Many children experience a pressure cooker effect – they need to tell and they want to keep the secret.

- Children need help to tell – they need an opportunity. Asking children questions about their psychological wellbeing provides them with this opportunity.

- Professional helpers can help children to tell, by understanding the complex reasons why children have difficulty telling, knowing the ways to help children tell and being there for children to help them along the pathway of disclosure.

- We need to take account of the child's context and the complex influences on the child when responding to concerns of sexual abuse.

CHAPTER 4

# Believing Children

Despite the growing awareness of sexual abuse, children continue to be afraid that if they tell someone they have been abused, they will not be believed. Sometimes this is founded and sometimes unfounded. Children can have difficulty believing what happened themselves. Some describe how unreal it seemed at the time, particularly when the abuse took place in the home and the adult continued to behave as if nothing had happened. Many older children and adults have described the belief that if they don't say it out loud they can avoid believing that it happened. Somehow, saying it out loud makes it real.

It is not unusual for parents and other adults to react to disclosure as if they don't believe it, that they can't quite believe that this could have happened. We do not want to believe that such a thing can have happened to a child – the very idea is 'unbelievable'. Many of the parents I interviewed described how unbelievable it was to hear that their child had been abused, even when they did not doubt that their child was telling the truth. Roland Summit[1] wrote how the 'protective denial surrounding sexual abuse can be seen as a natural consequence [of]... the need of almost all adults to insulate themselves from the painful realities of childhood victimization'. It is important to understand, therefore, that not believing can be a way of insulating ourselves to the awful reality of abuse.

Within a family, the consequences of believing that a child has been abused can lead to significant fallout. The child abuse investigations that ensue are stressful, intrusive and bring repercussions that extend

1   Summit (1983), p.179.

well beyond the nuclear family. When the abuser denies the abuse, families can be torn between believing the child and believing the abuser. When the person who abuses the child is an older sibling, parents may feel torn between believing their older child and their younger child, both of whom need their support and help.

Adults struggle with understanding why it is that children would not tell immediately if they are abused. Intuitively, it seems the most natural response to tell. As Summit notes: 'Unless specifically trained and sensitized, average adults…cannot believe that a normal, truthful child would tolerate incest without immediately reporting.'[2] When adults struggle with believing, when they react with shock and disbelief to children's disclosures, this can be interpreted by children as a sign that we do not believe them.

Parents also struggle with understanding why their child wouldn't tell them something like this immediately. It can be experienced as an insult to the parent–child relationship when a parent feels they have a good, trusting relationship with their child and that they are the first person their child can come to with a problem. Discovering that a child could not tell them can make a parent feel inadequate in their role as a parent or can undermine their ability to believe my child (how could the child keep something like this from me if it really happened?).

Some would caution against believing everything that children tell us, noting that such unquestioning faith in a child's story can be harmful, particularly if it turns out not to be true. The research shows that children rarely lie about sexual abuse. However, a child may lie in blaming one person for abusing them when they were abused by someone else, out of fear of the abuser. A child may want to get someone into trouble and not appreciate the seriousness of such an allegation. A child may fabricate a story about abuse as a way to get out of a difficult family situation. An adult may make a false allegation on behalf of a child against another adult, often a partner, as a means to prevent this partner having access to the child. A parent may genuinely believe that their child is being abused when they are not. A child may also be confused about the distinction

2  Summit (1983), p.186.

between knowing something because it happened to them or they have seen it happen, and knowing something because they have heard about this happening from someone else, or have seen it on a TV show or in a movie. Younger children in particular can be more compliant, less assertive and feel under pressure when asked questions by an adult, which can lead them to respond to questions by agreeing that things happened when this does not reflect reality. This is why it is so important to listen very carefully to children – paying attention to not only what they say but how they say it – and to get as much information as possible before forming an opinion about the credibility of what they are saying. I discuss this more in Chapter 5 when I talk about asking children questions.

This chapter will present the research findings on children's fears of not being believed, whether they were believed and how people reacted to their disclosures in terms of believing or not believing. I will then address why, as helpers, it can be difficult to believe children's accounts. The 'How to help' section will outline guidance for helpers in dealing with their own doubts and how they communicate with children, in particular during the early phase of disclosure when children are 'testing the waters' to see if the adult can be trusted with the information.

## What the research says

Unfortunately, despite increased awareness of the possibility of abuse and the prevalence of it in our society, children continue to describe concerns about being believed. In my own studies and those of others this was the most common theme identified. Through my interviews with children and young people, however, and from my interviews with parents and adults who had kept their secret for many years, I became aware of how complex this issue was.

### Children can doubt themselves that what happened actually happened

For most children it is something that they didn't even imagine happening. They have no term of reference for making sense of this experience. The context within which the abuse occurred – the syndrome of secrecy as Tilman Furniss described it – contributes not only to the need for secrecy but also to the 'unbelievable' nature of the experience. It is not talked about, so there is no opportunity for the child to speak out loud about their confusion and to have their beliefs and thoughts challenged. Children may be abused at night time in their own beds, when they are most defenceless, in which case they may question whether it really happened or whether it was just a bad dream. Furniss describes a typical context being a dark room, drawn curtains and no eye contact between the child and the abuser. This 'unreal quality' to the experience can add to a child's sense of the abuse not having occurred. A teenage girl I interviewed described the confusion caused by observing her abuser behaving towards her mother and siblings as if nothing had happened. This led her to question herself and also to wonder whether anyone would believe her. In this case, the abuser had told her that no one would believe her over him.

> He's just going on like nothing happened…and you're kinda, you know, you're sitting there saying: 'Is he for real? Am I imagining things? What's going on?'[3]

As children grow older, they often experience doubts about what happened. Their limited recall may exacerbate this doubt. Not telling may also contribute to the doubt. Keeping the secret can end up making people doubt their own story even more. In the words of Dympna (aged 16), 'the more you leave it unsaid the more unbelievable it becomes'. Dympna said she didn't really believe it was happening until she said it to a friend:

> Cos it's a crazy, it is a crazy situation…cos I never believed it for a long long time until I actually told me friends and they were like: 'Listen, you know what I mean, this is major.'[4]

---

3   McElvaney (2015b), p.158.
4   McElvaney (2015b), p.158.

## Children can be threatened that they won't be believed

Children who are vulnerable – due to their mental health or other disability – are more vulnerable to being abused and more vulnerable in terms of not telling anyone about the abuse. Rianach (aged 15) described how her mother's partner told her that no one would believe her if she told them about what happened:

> That because I'm on tablets for depression and used to cut myself that I'm not in a state of mind to say what happened to a judge.[5]

Eilis (aged 18) was abused by the father and son in a family where she was living. She told the mother, who physically beat her. Eilis did not question whether the woman believed her or not – she was punishing her for saying it.

> The wife used to tell me like: 'There's no one you're gonna tell that's going to believe you.'[6]

This woman was probably right. Who would believe that this upstanding man and his son were raping this young girl on a weekly basis? Eilis described her abusers as being from a very respectable family in the community. The father was a man of status in that community, 'then there's me, tiny me, saying something'. Even in the absence of explicit threats not to tell, when the abuser is someone known to the family and liked by the family, children can fear that they will not be believed. One girl described her brother not believing her when she said that her sister's husband abused her:

> He told me that [alleged abuser] wouldn't do that.

---

5   McElvaney (2015b), p.161.
6   McElvaney (2015b), p.161.

## Often children want to forget about what happened

This forgetting can range from not consciously thinking about the abuse experience to the more extreme experience of dissociation that is an unconscious way of putting out of one's mind experiences that cannot be emotionally tolerated. We all exercise the coping strategy of putting things out of our minds: 'I don't want to think about that now, I'll think about it later when I feel more able to.' In the extreme case, we are not aware of putting the experience out of our mind, it just happens. In the first instance, we can easily recall the experience if someone or something reminds us of it. In the case of dissociation, the experience is out of our awareness and it can be difficult to access the memory of the experience. Many authors describe dissociation as an adaptive way of coping with overwhelming emotional trauma.[7]

## Children often fear that they will not be believed

The fear of not being believed has been noted in research as preventing children from telling. Young people can be exceptionally good at predicting adults' reactions to their disclosure. In some studies, when young people expected not to be believed, they were not believed.[8] However, young people can have these concerns without foundation. One young girl I interviewed said:

> They believed me straight away so to me that was a big thing because that was my main worry... I used to always think that people would never believe me – that was kind of one of the main reasons why I never told anybody but everybody did.[9]

Another young person did expect to be believed and wasn't:

> I thought family members would believe me but turned out they were the worst.

7 Bentovim (1992); Rogers (2006).
8 Hershkowitz *et al.* (2007).
9 McElvaney (2015b), pp.159–160.

## Sometimes children are not believed

One study noted that of a total of 193 families, 22 per cent of mothers did not believe their children.[10] In this study, the mother was less likely to believe the child if the abuser was a boyfriend or the child's stepfather than if he was a member of the extended family or if it was the child's father. Mothers were less likely to believe their child when they reported more intrusive abuse – such as intercourse. Younger children were more likely to be believed than older children. Finally, mothers were less likely to believe the child if the abuse was reported as taking place when the mother was in the home.

There is, in my view, a misperception that in the past parents didn't believe their children when they disclosed sexual abuse ('in them days just nobody would believe you')[11] and that parents and others are more believing of children nowadays. Rita (aged 35) described how she told her mother immediately about a dentist who abused her at her dental appointment:

> I'll never forget it. It was horrible – he was trying to kiss me and everything. I don't know how I got away [but] I did and I went home and I told my mother and she says: 'How dare you talk about that nice man like that.' She wouldn't believe me, you know.[12]

Many are of the view that with the increased awareness of the issue in recent decades, this is no longer a problem in our society. This, unfortunately, is not the case and does not take account of the complex situation parents are faced with when a child begins to disclose that they have been abused.

Young people have described being interviewed by police, feeling that they were not viewed as reliable and that the policemen did not believe them.[13] This appeared to be related to the extent of questioning ('I had a feeling of the policeman not believing me, he asked me

---

10  Sirles and Frank (1989).
11  McElvaney (2015b), p.161.
12  McElvaney (2015b), p.161.
13  Back *et al.* (2011).

so many questions') and the style of questioning, challenging what the children were saying about the sexual abuse. The children noted that a good relationship with the police interviewer was important to help them to tell their story. They also described their experience in court as difficult ('the questions he asked me so aggressively and stupidly…and he had his own answers since he did not believe in me') and disrespectful ('I understand that it is his job but I cannot understand that he must insult me'). They described doubting themselves when challenged by defence counsel as to why accounts given by the child in differing contexts (police statement vs. court) differed ('They try to crack me so I will begin to say things which are not true and so I will be just confused – I did not know if it was I myself who had done wrong'). They also described feeling relieved and satisfied when they left court but also feeling that they were not believed and that they were held responsible for the abuse.

Young people have also described how professionals didn't believe them when they disclosed sexual abuse and how this impacted on their motivation to tell anyone else.[14]

## Parents can respond to children with doubt

Sometimes this comes from actual doubt that the child is telling the truth – the parent may assume the child must have misunderstood or that the child is imagining it or that they are telling a lie to get the person into trouble for some unknown reason. Ramona Alaggia[15] has written about how mothers' responses in believing and not believing need to be better understood, in particular the pressure that mothers feel under from professionals and their social networks. Mothers can feel isolated following disclosures. They can blame themselves for not noticing the abuse sooner and they can be blamed by others for not preventing it.

---

14 Tucker (2011).
15 Alaggia (2002).

## Delays in disclosure can undermine children's credibility

Anna Salter[16] described the dilemma for children who are caught up in a 'Catch 22' situation if they do not disclose immediately. When children are being groomed for sexual abuse, the behaviour may be difficult to categorize as abuse. The abuser may be quite subtle in gradually breaching boundaries, so that the child feels uncomfortable about what is happening but is not sure how to communicate this to others, perhaps not wanting to be seen as overreacting. However, when the abuse develops into something more clearly abusive, the child feels responsible for going along with it, for not telling sooner. They feel more culpable at this stage and more caught up in keeping the secret.

As noted in Chapter 3, most children delay in disclosing. Young people are well aware of how this delay can make people question their credibility. According to Aine (aged 17), if you were abused when you were six and you didn't say until you were 20:

> No one would believe you… They'd say: 'What took so long to tell?'

Deirdre (aged 18) also believed that the delay in telling would make it difficult for her parents to believe her:

> It's not that I didn't trust my Mam and Dad, it's just I didn't know what they were gonna think and I didn't know what they were gonna think about me not telling them before.

Summit first wrote about this in 1983, highlighting how the delay in telling contributing to people's disbelief. Adults were convinced that if such a thing happened to a child, they would tell someone immediately. Adults who were abused in childhood have described how they would anticipate people responding if they first tell as adults – for example, as Christina (aged 52) put it:

> And why didn't I come forward, why didn't I report this years ago?

---

16  Salter (1995).

## The psychological impact of the abuse

This can in itself contribute to delays in telling, which in turn undermine children's credibility. Getting into trouble in school or acting out socially can also make young people feel that people will not believe them. Deirdre (aged 18) explains how she 'got a bit off the wall – my behaviour was crazy' and this made her afraid that her parents wouldn't believe her.

## When adults don't believe children, this can lead to the child recanting the allegation

One young person I interviewed disclosed to her mother, then recanted, then disclosed again. She described how her mother believed her but her grandmother persisted in asking her whether she was sure. In fact, her mother had doubted whether she was telling the truth as there had been dissent in the home and the mother was concerned that the daughter was using this as a way to get back at her partner. When she recanted, she described how everybody so easily believed that the abuse had not happened and that they were relieved things could go back to normal. Her mother's partner moved back into the home and the social workers left them alone. However, in my interview with her mother, she described how she remained watchful of the tension between her daughter and her partner, and her daughter's protectiveness of her. When her daughter later disclosed again, her mother experienced no doubts – she knew then that her daughter was telling the truth. Young people are more likely to recant when there is a lack of support in the family.[17] Lovett described young people's 'inability to foresee that things within the family will get better with time' (p.358).

## Families can move between believing and not believing and back again

A young person I interviewed was abused by her sister's boyfriend one night when she was babysitting for the couple. She disclosed

---

17 Lovett (2004).

the abuse immediately to her sister and her sister unhesitatingly believed her, even insisting that it be reported to the police. The girl was reluctant, however, and did not want her mother to find out. Then, over the course of the next few days, the sister withdrew her support and when their mother found out, the sister defended her partner, to the point that it caused a rift in the family. At the time I interviewed the mother, she had not seen her daughter or grandchildren in over a year.

## Children can forget that they were abused

In the opening lines of her autobiography, *I Know Why the Caged Bird Sings*, Maya Angelou describes how 'I hadn't so much forgot as I couldn't bring myself to remember.'[18] There is a lot of misinformation about memory and children – for example, that children cannot remember experiences they had at an early age or that children's memories are more unreliable than adults' memories. Some children do have difficulty recalling experiences, while others give remarkably accurate details that can be corroborated by others of experiences they had at a very early age. The research shows that children can be just as reliable as adults in their memories, but younger children in particular are more vulnerable to being influenced by conversations with adults or being asked questions by adults that 'put ideas into their heads'.

Bessel van der Kolk, a psychiatrist in Boston, was one of the first to recognize that the reason why some people have visceral memories is because their state of shock at the time of the trauma influenced how they encoded the information into their memory system. He referred to implicit memory and explicit memory. Implicit memory is where information is encoded by the limbic system of our brains, bypassing the prefrontal cortex, the part of the brain that is sometimes referred to as our 'thinking brain'. It's as if the experience is uploaded directly as an image into our brain rather than an experience that we have understood. It's a little like the difference between rote learning and understanding a concept.

---

18  Angelou (1984), p.3.

We can reproduce something without actually understanding it. We can access memories as discrete pictures or sensations, without being able to make any sense of them. This is because they were uploaded as an implicit memory rather than as an explicit memory.

Another related concept relevant to remembering and forgetting sexual abuse experiences is repression. Alaggia describes the scepticism of adults about repression: 'How can they forget something so horrible?'[19] It's actually because it is so horrible that it's possible to forget it. It is important to distinguish here between suppression (consciously putting something out of our mind) and represssion, an unconscious process. We choose to 'forget about' things that we don't want to think about. When we choose to think about them again, this is not a 'recovered memory' but a taking down off the shelf and dusting off some old cast-aside memory that we haven't wanted to look at for a long time. The term 'recovered memory' refers to a memory that a person was not consciously aware of, that was repressed (an unconscious process as distinct from a deliberate conscious process) and that has been brought into consciousness and awareness, usually unwillingly. We all experience these processes. When we meet up with old friends who we haven't seen in years and chat about old times, these conversations can bring into the foreground of awareness memories that we haven't thought about for a long time, helping us to remember things we had forgotten. The theory behind repression is that we cannot face the pain of remembering certain experiences, so we 'repress' them or push them beyond our awareness to protect us from that pain. By erasing the memory, we don't feel the pain.

When these memories resurface, they are usually accompanied by emotional pain, which at the time may feel unbearable. In a way, it is unbearable – it couldn't be tolerated previously and so it was repressed. Memories like these may be triggered when a person engages in psychotherapy and begins to talk about long-forgotten experiences, thus opening up the path to the unconscious. We all know the experience of when we begin to talk about our childhood, we begin to remember more and more. This is normal remembering.

---

19 Alaggia (2004), p.1222.

When repressed memories come into consciousness, they can be experienced as traumatic and manifest themselves in the form of flashbacks, intrusive unwanted thoughts or images of difficult experiences that we have had. People may not recognize these flashbacks as memories initially. It may take time for them to accept and allow the memories to come back as coherent stories, as such memories typically don't have a beginning, middle and end. They weren't stored (encoded) like this so they are not recalled (retrieved) like this.

## Children can lie about sexual abuse

In a very small proportion of instances, children have been found to say they have been abused when they haven't or allege that one person abused them when they were being abused by someone else. There is a lot of concern about the issue of 'false allegations'. While it is difficult to 'prove' that sexual abuse has occurred, it is arguably even more difficult to prove that it has not occurred. In the absence of incontrovertible evidence that there has been sexual abuse, someone can live their life with suspicion hanging over them that is almost impossible to clear.

# Minding myself

The first step for the professional helper in being able to respond to concerns about sexual abuse is that *we educate ourselves* about the phenomenon of sexual abuse, how it happens, the various ways that children can be groomed into this interaction and the impact that it can have on children, their families, and the child's wider social context. When people have limited exposure, and therefore limited awareness of the occurrence of sexual abuse, this makes it more difficult for them to believe. Dympna (aged 16) captures this well:

> It's not that people don't love you. I think it's just if they haven't dealt with something like this before, they probably wouldn't understand or, you know, know what to do.

The second step is that *we keep an open mind* and be prepared to accept that anything is possible. We can all identify with the idea of not wanting to believe that something terrible has happened and we all have different ways of dealing with this. One of these ways is to 'shut it out' or not think about it, thus keeping some distance between us and reality. This is a useful coping strategy and has served many people well when dealing with intolerable situations. Nevertheless, awareness of our belief systems about the occurrence of sexual abuse, children's memory abilities and our desire not to think about abuse impacts on our ability to believe children when they tell us they have been abused.

A common reaction to hearing about a sexual abuse concern is to search for an alternative explanation. Perhaps the child misunderstood? Perhaps the behaviour wasn't intentional? It is difficult to accept that people abuse children. Somehow it reflects on all of us human beings that someone among us has the capacity to hurt a child in this way. When this is someone we know, and perhaps even like or love, the tendency to seek other explanations is even stronger. The mother of Joe (aged 8) described how she couldn't believe what her son was trying to tell her, not that she thought he was telling lies but rather that she thought that her son had misunderstood a situation.

> He said to me, 'Em Mammy [alleged abuser] touched my bum', and I was a bit embarrassed at first. He just said it out and there was a busload of people and then I kinda just went, 'What are you saying things like that for', you know? I just said: 'Well, maybe it was an accident when he was going to look for you.' Like I was presuming this game what he was describing like hide and seek… I just kinda, I put it down to an innocent thing that a child would do.

She thought her son was describing an incident with a child of the same age:

> At the time so I was placing in my head that it was a ten-year-old that did this and that maybe it was an innocent thing as in he was behind a door or under a bed or something

and he grabbed him and he put his hand on his bum and he made [Joe] feel uncomfortable and that was why he told me.

However, her son told her the next day of another incident:

First of all, I was like I couldn't believe like. I was freaking it in my head, I was going ballistic but I was like, right, I got him to say it again because I couldn't believe the first time.

She described telling her husband:

I had to tell [husband] ten times before it registered.

Sexual abuse doesn't just happen to other children in other situations. Even allowing for the most conservative of estimates, if we translate this into our own context, any helper that is involved with a group of at least ten children is likely to be in the company of at least one child who has been abused, is being abused or will be abused. We need to accept this reality, both intellectually and emotionally, and be prepared for the possibility that on any day at any time, we may be confronted with concerns about a child that we need to act on.

The third step is that *we ensure we have support* – someone we can talk to about our concerns, our attitudes, our prejudices, our instinctive reactions; someone we can bounce ideas off as to how to deal with the situation. The one thing we should never do when we are concerned about a child is keep it to ourselves. The secretive nature of sexual abuse has tentacles that reach out well beyond the abuser and the abused. It stretches out to helpers and the entire system that responds: the child protection system and the legal system. We can collude with the secrecy surrounding sexual abuse by not expressing our concerns about a child. We can rationalize this by thinking 'oh, maybe I misheard' or 'maybe I'm overreacting' or 'I don't want to blow this up into something it's not'. These are all valid concerns. However, if we stay with what we've noticed, and avoid jumping to conclusions about what this means; if we describe the behaviour or what the child said and we stay as close as possible to their words and what we see and avoid putting any interpretation on that, we won't be jumping to conclusions. It could mean anything but it always means something.

# How to help

I encourage helpers to take a believing stance – that it is best to accept what a child says, to encourage them to talk more about it and to reserve judgement about the 'truth' or otherwise until more information has been gathered. It is important not to jump to conclusions too quickly and it is important to give a child space to say more.

## Facilitating awareness

Sometimes children don't understand that behaviour is abusive. If children have never heard of such an experience and if they don't know of any other child who has had this experience, it is difficult for them to be able to make sense of what is happening when they are abused. Also, the grooming that is so typical of the process of sexual abuse means that the abusive behaviour is only gradually introduced. Initially, the behaviour can be quite benign while the abuser is nurturing a relationship with the child. It can be difficult for anyone – child or adult – to discern that this is abusive behaviour or that it is a precedent to abusive behaviour. It is often only as it develops that the situation becomes clearer. It is our responsibility as adults to help educate children to trust their feelings and to tell us when someone makes them feel uncomfortable.

We need to convey messages to children that we can believe anything, we are open to the possibility that abuse has occurred and we will not be shocked to the extent that we do not believe. It is important for children to be understood and to be able to make sense of their world in order to feel safe. When children are confused and don't understand what's going on, they feel unsafe.

What children need most is containment. They need to know that we will be able to manage whatever they throw at us. This does not mean looking for evidence of abuse where none exists. It does, however, mean listening to the warning signals and being able to hear them when children try to communicate in ways that are not so clear and easy to decipher.

As professional helpers we have an obligation that goes beyond helping children themselves become more aware of the possibility of abuse occurring. Given the extent to which young people describe not being believed by parents, friends and people in their community, we have an obligation to educate the wider community about the possibility of abuse and the importance of listening to and believing children when they tell us about difficult experiences.

## Facilitating expression

Having conversations about the possibility of abuse conveys a message to a child that we are open to believing that such things happen. News reports on the radio or TV about sexual abuse, and films or TV programmes that feature the issue of child sexual abuse can provide such opportunities. Taking a 'believing stance' in our interactions with children about everyday events helps to build up trust in children that we will believe them when they tell us something. While I discuss in Chapter 6 the importance of asking children questions about their emotional wellbeing to encourage them to engage in conversations, it is also important to appreciate that if a child tells us something that has happened we need to be careful not to ask too many questions. The nature of our questioning can lead children to believe that we are questioning their credibility. One girl I interviewed described how her grandmother kept asking her 'Are you sure?' after she disclosed that her mother's partner was abusing her. She described feeling under pressure as a result of these questions. Why would her grandmother keep asking if she believed her?

Children may need help in putting words to their experiences. As noted earlier, saying it out loud may help the child believe it themselves but children may not have the words to articulate their experiences. As helpers, we need to teach children the language of emotional expression: how to verbally communicate their distress and the reasons for their distress. This can be a language for emotions – 'happy', 'sad', 'upset', 'confused', 'afraid'; it can be a language for good touches and bad touches – 'sore', 'yucky', 'embarrassing', 'touches that make me feel good', 'touches that make me feel uncomfortable'; it can be a language for children's rights – 'I need', 'I deserve', 'that is bold/wrong', 'no one should hurt me'.

We need to take a stance that conveys a strong message that we are interested, curious, non-judgemental and able to hear whatever the child wants or needs to tell us. When a child feels that a professional wants to hear more, this will encourage them to feel that they can trust us and this will help them to say more. We need to foster clear communication, by being good role models in how we communicate with children, by checking with them that we have understood them correctly. We need to be careful not to jump to conclusions too quickly. Our anxiety can cloud our judgements. Fears for children can get in the way of understanding clearly what children are telling us.

## Facilitating action

Through our actions, we demonstrate to children that we believe them. While helpers need to be cautious, this caution should never get in the way of doing something about our concerns. In the first instance, this may simply be speaking to another colleague about the concern. Letting a child know that we are going to speak to someone else about the concern tells the child that we are taking it seriously and that we are doing something about it. Children may seek promises from a helper not to tell anyone about what they are saying. In this instance, it is important for the helper to reassure the child that it would not be appropriate to make this kind of promise; that it is important for us to speak with our colleagues when we are worried about something. Children can be concerned that as helpers we will act on the information in such a way that the child loses control of the situation. As I discussed in Chapter 3, containing the secret of the abuse can be the way the child copes with the psychological fallout from the abuse. If they keep the secret, they can maintain control over what happens next. However, this control is too much of a burden for children to carry. While they may feel the need to keep control, it may not be in their best interests to do so. As adults and as helpers it is our responsibility to take this burden from them and to take action as appropriate.

We will all have guidelines that we are required to follow in such instances. This may come from our employer or from national policies and procedures. It is our responsibility as helpers to ensure that we are aware of such policies and procedures and that we know who we need to go to when we need guidance in such situations.

We are not helping children by believing something that is not true. The harm that we can do by not believing a child when they are telling the truth must be avoided at the same time as not reinforcing a child's misperception or misunderstanding of behaviour that was not abuse. The best way to deal with this is to listen to the child and encourage them to say as much as possible; we should also accept the child's perspective, allowing them to lead, and remain open to understanding and making sense of the situation with the child. When children are vague and we feel a growing sense of concern, it is important that we remain calm ourselves so that we do not interfere with the child's account. We must be open to the possibility that a child has been abused at the same time as we remain open to the possibility that there is another explanation for what a child is telling us or signalling to us through their behaviour.

## Key messages

- Children can doubt their own experiences and find it hard to believe that they have been/are being abused.

- Adults can doubt children – because they find it hard to believe such a thing could have happened, because they can't face up to the reality themselves and because they don't trust children.

- Fear of not being believed and the experience of not being believed can prevent children from telling, leaving them at significant risk of further abuse and mental health difficulties.

- We must be open to the possibility of abuse if we are going to be able to believe children when they tell us they have been abused.

- We need to actively communicate to children that we can be trusted and that we will believe them when they tell us about their concerns.

- We need to act on the information we get from children and inform them that we are doing something about it.

- Children can feel relieved when they tell us their concerns and we believe them. Taking action on what they tell us communicates to them that they are believed.

# CHAPTER 5

# Recognizing the Signs

This chapter focuses on recognizing signs that children may have been abused. Many helpers ask the question: 'How would I know that a child is being abused?' The answer is: 'We don't.' However, we can – and must – consider the possibility. We can – and must – closely observe and monitor children's presentations. And we can – and must – act on these observations. There is no 'litmus test' for sexual abuse. There are few, if any, behavioural or emotional indicators that are definitive evidence that sexual abuse has occurred. There was a time when children's sexualized behaviour or sexual knowledge beyond their developmental age set off alarm bells for adults, signalling that perhaps the child had been abused. Unfortunately, with the increased availability of sexually explicit materials in print, on television and through the internet; with the increased use of sexual language among young children in the playground or the school yard (even if they don't understand the words they are using); and with the increase in sexualized behaviour among children, these 'signs' are no longer considered to be indicative of sexual abuse. Children can engage in sexualized behaviour to imitate something they have observed, they can use sexualized behaviour as a form of dominating other children – as a form of bullying – and they can engage in such behaviours as a means of seeking comfort or excitement. Or they may engage in sexual behaviour that imitates something that has been done to them.

Nevertheless, children often signal through their behaviour that all is not right in their world. This can show in the form of psychosomatic complaints – tummy aches, headaches, aches and pains, nausea or a general lethargy. Children who were previously outgoing may become quiet and withdrawn; children who were typically quiet and shy may become irritable and appear troublesome. Changes in children's typical behaviour can be a sign that something is wrong.

Children often communicate their distress through emotional signs rather than verbally. Parents describe themselves as having a 'radar'. They know when something is off with their child because they are tuned into them, they are familiar with their moods and their behaviour and so they notice when children are fearful or avoidant or something has happened that is bothering them. Professional helpers, in the same way, become attuned to children that they know and work with. Over time we get to know them and their little idiosyncrasies, and we become sensitive to changes in the child's behaviour or emotional state. It is always important to make note of fearful or avoidant responses to an individual, be that an adult or an older child, or even a child of the same age. What we are looking for is a pattern. The first time we notice a child appearing fearful, we may not think this is a cause of concern. The second time, we may recall noticing this before. Now is the time to make a note of it – a note of the current concern and the fact that this was noticed on a previous occasion.

In this chapter I will focus on what we know about the psychological impact on children who have been abused and use this information to highlight in particular the non-verbal indicators that a child may be experiencing sexual abuse. Knowing about psychological impact helps to inform us of what signs to look out for, taking care not to over-interpret or jump to conclusions. The section on 'Minding myself' addresses how our own experiences (or lack of experiences) can lead us to misinterpret children's behaviour and gives advice on what we need to do to make sure that this does not get in the way of how we talk with children about these behaviours. Guidance is offered on how to facilitate communication when as helpers we notice something in a child's behaviour or presentation that raises alarm bells for us in relation to sexual abuse.

## What the research says

Many children try to tell through their behaviour or other non-verbal communication before they are able to articulate their experiences. Most children don't purposefully tell, and even when they do, even when we talk with them about why it is that they told on that particular day or to that particular person, it is often not clear what prompted them to do it.

> I never actually planned to turn round and tell somebody. I never said, 'Right, today's the day I'm gonna tell somebody cos I tried for so long to tell'... I never actually knew why I turned around and said, '[Boyfriend], this is what actually happened to me'...but I suppose everything just builds up an' then finally just comes out.[1]

Debbie Allnock and Pam Miller[2] interviewed young adults about their experiences of disclosure and help-seeking. They identified key messages relating to the child, the family, the community and the school as to why the abuse didn't stop sooner.

- Children don't have the knowledge or a reference point to recognize that the abuse is wrong.

- Family members don't notice the signs of abuse. When they do, they aren't willing to act.

- Neighbours don't report their concern and aren't sure where to turn to when they are willing to.

- Education staff don't notice the signs of abuse and are too quick to label the children as 'troublesome'.

Clearly, awareness is key: children's awareness of what constitutes abuse and others' ability to recognize the signs of abuse and be prepared to do something about it.

One young girl described how she was kept home at times to work and missed school. Her teachers noticed her absences and

---

1   McElvaney (2015b), p.140.
2   Allnock and Miller (2013), p.49.

would ask her from time to time: 'What's wrong?' She never told them. She noted:

> Teachers don't want to meddle because there's no social work there, not like your child is your child whatever happens that's your child, so it's kind of not really no one's business.

One of her teachers did show concern and would send the child to buy lunch for her, and then when she returned, the teacher would ask her to eat it herself as she was clearly concerned that she was being neglected.

A 15-year-old boy I interviewed described how his school helped him tell. His school work had been deteriorating over the previous few months and he had got into trouble a few times with his class tutor for not having his homework done or not having his school books with him. This was out of character for him as he had been very well behaved and studious prior to this. He described how one day he was caught smoking in school and his tutor brought him to the office. The tutor wanted to ring his mother and father as he could smell the smoke on him. His parents didn't know he smoked and he was worried about getting into trouble with them. He said his tutor was wondering what was wrong with him, asking him why he was acting like this. He broke down, saying: 'You don't understand, you don't know what I've been through.' His teacher asked him: 'What exactly have you been through?' He told the teacher that his cousin had abused him many years previously. He said his teacher didn't believe him at first, saying: 'Come on, tell me what…tell me what happened.' The teacher then took him to see the principal. The principal listened to his story and told him to come back the next day when they'd 'sort something out'. The following day when he returned to the principal, the principal told the boy that he would have to tell his mother within the next three weeks or the principal would have to call his parents in. The boy was terrified. This was six years after the onset of the abuse. He was 15. However, by the end of the three-week deadline, he had told his older brother, who helped him to tell his parents.

# What are the signs to look out for?

In Chapter 2, I described the psychological impact on the child of being sexually abused. If we take these various impacts, and think about how this might be manifested in a child's behaviour or mood or general way of being, this can help us to notice the signs that something is wrong.

*Stigmatization* is similar to the concept of the '*damaged goods syndrome*', where children internalize the bad feelings from the bad experience of abuse. This might show in a child's poor opinion of themselves. We might notice a child running themselves down all the time or indicating that they are no good at anything, or that somehow the child does not believe he is a good person. Children may feel 'different' because of the abuse. This can make them feel dirty or damaged in some way. As many feel guilty or ashamed of being abused, they may feel that they are bad. This feeling of badness is internalized and undermines the child's self-esteem. Children also often feel isolated and alone in the world, not aware that other children have had similar experiences. They often believe that if people knew the truth about them, they would not want anything to do with them.

*Betrayal* refers to the betrayal of *trust* that the child experiences when they have been abused. This may take many forms. A child may experience depression or grief reactions at the loss of a trusted figure when they are abused by someone they know and like, perhaps even love. Their trust has been shattered and this can extend to not being able to trust other people in their life. Children may appear *fearful*. Children can suddenly appear wary or cautious around adults where they previously were open and trusting. They may be afraid of the abuser and this may show in their behaviour of wanting to avoid contact with someone. They may have been threatened that something terrible will happen if they do not go along with the abuse or if they tell. This may manifest as anxious behaviour in that the child becomes anxious in their everyday life – anxious about going to school, anxious about homework and anxious about playing with friends. Anxiety can take many forms in childhood. Children may have difficulty sleeping – they may fear going to sleep, they may have nightmares, they may wake up in the night and be fearful of falling back to sleep again or be fearful of the dark or of being alone.

At the other end of the spectrum, children may react to the loss of trust by intensifying their need to trust others, thus trusting strangers they don't even know. This need for trust can be seen as a need for security, but children can seek this out in ways that are not helpful for them. Children may become clingy, not wanting to separate. Alternatively, children may become angry and hostile, mistrusting adult figures that they rely on. This can be their way of protecting themselves from being hurt again or it may be a manifestation of feeling angry that the abuse happened and wanting to fight back against the world. They can be seen as 'troublesome' by adults and so get cut off from the supports they so desperately need in order to be able to tell about the abuse. Children may experience difficulties in their peer relationships that are based on a lack of trust.

Children may experience *low mood*, become withdrawn and quiet, and appear sad. Low mood can manifest itself through psychosomatic symptoms such as tummy pains or headaches. Children may suffer a lot from physical illness and pick up infections easily because their immune system is not functioning well under the stress of the psychological impact of the abuse. The withdrawing into themselves can impact on children's social skills and they may appear more reluctant to go out with their friends. They may be less engaging when they are with their friends and may have difficulty standing up for themselves in socially challenging situations with peers. Children may have *difficulty regulating their emotions*, particularly their anger. They may appear irritable and have a low frustration tolerance threshold, getting angry at the slightest thing and appearing angry for no apparent reason.

Children can experience *confusion with role boundaries*: they may appear to want to look after people when this is not appropriate – for example, when it goes beyond being considerate or kind and moves into the territory of taking responsibility for other people, particularly in relation to parents. When children appear to have a need to look after their parents, it can be a temporary situation when a parent is unwell. If this persists, it may reflect a difficulty with roles in the family, where the child is taking on responsibilities that should rest with the parent. Children can appear to be *mature and yet immature* at the same time. They may appear 'grown up' and still struggle with developmental tasks appropriate to their age level. Finally, a child can struggle with *being in control* – being able to manage themselves and cope with everyday ups and downs.

*Traumatic sexualization* refers to the impact that sexual abuse can have on a child's sexual development. Young children can be *preoccupied with sexuality*, shown through repetitive sexual behaviour or masturbation or fascination with body parts – their own and other people's. Children can act out sexually in their play with other children. Children may use phrases or appear to have sexual knowledge that is beyond their years – references to intercourse or oral–genital contact. Children may act out aggressively with other children – either same-age school friends or younger children. Older children may appear to be uncomfortable when watching sex scenes on TV programmes. They may appear unduly embarrassed when conversations about sex take place in the classroom or in groups of young people. They may experience difficulties with intimacy in romantic relationships or they may appear overly promiscuous and unaware of social boundaries when it comes to sexual behaviour. Older children can struggle with body image as they reach puberty and experience changes in their bodies. They may also struggle with sexual feelings as this may remind them of the abuse and they may associate any sexual arousal with the experience of abuse. The experience of sexual abuse may introduce the child to sexual feelings and thoughts at a time when they are not developmentally ready to manage such feelings and understand such thoughts. Older children may be confronted with questions about their sexual identity. If a boy is abused by a man, the boy may have questions about why he was selected for abuse: 'Am I gay?' Sometimes older children may become overly self-conscious, wondering if people can tell by looking at them that they have been abused. Younger children can confuse affection with sexual abuse and seek this out in other relationships, leading to a view of them as promiscuous and inappropriate. Children may feel disgusted about what happened, and therefore sexual contact as they mature may be associated with negative feelings – disgust, anger, fear and the sense of powerlessness. This can develop into an aversion to sexual intimacy that they may struggle with as adults.

*Powerlessness* affects children in different ways. It can be seen in children's fear and anxiety, their inability to feel that they have any control over themselves or their lives and what happens to them. Children's sense of efficacy can be affected. When children are abused over a period of time, they can develop an expectation that they will be abused repeatedly. It undermines a child's sense of efficacy, impairing their sense of themselves as competent human beings. Particularly when children are abused over a period of time or on different occasions, they can lose a sense that they have any power over what happens to them. This can lead to a *belief of impotence*, that they will always be a victim and that there is nothing they can do about it, which can impact on the child in terms of feeling *depressed, despairing and even suicidal*. It can impact on children's ability to engage in peer activities as they do not believe they are competent in any way – in sports and in school work – so they give up trying. This powerlessness can also impact on the child's ability to protect themselves from other abusive behaviour such as bullying or further abuse. The powerlessness can make them an easy target for others to abuse. Some children will try to compensate for this feeling of powerlessness by *being abusive to others* – bullying other children, being violent and getting into trouble. The wish to have control over others or to dominate them can stem from a feeling of being out of control, of not having any control over their own self or life. Being abusive to others can give children a sense of power that they do not otherwise feel and can in its own way be that child's way of coping with the aftermath of abuse.

## Minding myself

As helpers, we need to be aware of how *our own experience or lack of experience impacts on our ability to recognize the possible signs of sexual abuse*. If we have had difficult experiences in childhood, we may want to put these behind us so much that we are blind to the possibility that a child has been abused. We may have never faced up to the reality of what happened to us or the impact that it had on us. We may not have acknowledged that perhaps it did do us harm. Helpers who have not worked through their own issues arising from their experiences of abuse are more at risk of not being able to pick up the warning signs from children that something is going on. Their way of coping with their own history gets in the way of protecting children. They might even place children, unwittingly, in more risky situations as a result of this 'blindness' as they are not as good at recognizing risky situations. They don't allow themselves to go there. In some cases, even when the evidence is very clear that a child has been abused, they still don't believe it. Their huge need to protect themselves from the reality of their own pain results in them rejecting the child, that is, insisting that the child misunderstood or blatantly blaming the child for making it up.

At the other end of the spectrum, there are helpers who have their own history of abuse and are supersensitive to the possibility that a child might be abused, to the extent that they jump too quickly to the assumption that abuse has taken place. They interpret behaviour as indicative of abuse when there are countless other explanations for this behaviour. They are closed to those other possibilities.

Having a history of abuse may mean that a helper is very uncomfortable talking with a child about abuse because the conversation triggers their own distress, reminds them of the experience they had and opens up uncomfortable feelings about that experience. This can get in the way of being able to listen to a child. It can affect how we hear children: we may only hear the similarities with our own experience and not notice the differences between the child's experience and ours. We may assume the child feels about their abuse the same way as we felt or even now feel about what happened to us. Our judgement can therefore be clouded by our own experience. At the other extreme, having had an experience of abuse may mean that we are more able to have this conversation with children. Because we are familiar with these experiences, we may be more comfortable with this conversation and less shocked that such a thing could happen because we know from our own experience that it does. We may thus be more able to listen, knowing how individual the experience is and how differently we all react to such experiences. Having had the experience can thus make us either less able to tolerate the child's distress or more able to tolerate it.

The important skill is to be able to recognize how we are with these conversations. We need to be aware of how we feel about the issue. We need to be aware of our own 'blind spots'. We need to recognize that we are going to find a conversation upsetting. And we need to be able to either remove ourselves from the situation or change the subject in such a way that we do not give the child the message that what they are talking about is 'unmanageable'. It is very easy for a child to get the message that the adult is not able to hear this terrible thing, and this may make them harder to reach. Many young people and adults have described difficult experiences they had when they tried to tell a professional helper and I discuss this further in Chapter 9. Part of this is to do with the level of comfort we feel as helpers in talking about sexual issues and sexual abuse.

When I described in Chapter 3 the pressure cooker effect that children experience and the pull between wanting and not wanting to tell, one issue that struck me was young people's expectation that parents and other adults would know by the way they behaved that they were being abused. An unfortunate consequence when adults did not pick up on the signals was that young people felt that the adults didn't care. Deirdre (aged 18) recalls:

> I was depressed... I got a bit off the wall. My behaviour was crazy – that's why me and my Mam used to fight an awful lot cos I would kinda think: 'How do you not know?' D'ya know what I mean? ... 'Why don't you, why don't you try and find out what's going on?' And then I thought: 'Oh, cos she doesn't care, cos that, cos I'm a bad person.'

# How to help
## Facilitating awareness
When we notice a child's emotional state, this helps them to notice it and be aware of it. By paying attention to children, getting to know them and noticing when things change, we can help children become aware of how they feel about what is happening to them. By drawing attention to their emotional state, we show them that we care, that we notice and that we want to do something to help

them. Ordinary, everyday comments such as 'I notice you're a bit down today', 'I noticed you were upset earlier' and 'You're not yourself today' can help a child feel seen and noticed and give them the message that there is someone there who will listen to them if they need help. Listening with our eyes and our ears will help us become attuned to a child's emotional state. We can use our own senses to pick up on how a child is feeling. By feeding that back to the child, we can help the child put words to how they are feeling. We may get it wrong, but our efforts do not go unnoticed. Getting it wrong gives us an opportunity to try again and keep trying.

Teaching children about boundaries (what is okay and not okay), their right to protection and safety, healthy and unhealthy relationships, and how to get help when needed helps make children aware of abuse when it does occur.

## Facilitating expression

Children often hint or give what we call 'partial disclosures' to 'test the waters' with helpers. They may be cautious about whether they can trust us, and are watching for the response they get before deciding whether they can take the next step and say more. Knowing this helps us to consider the possibility that any communication can be a little hint that something is not right. Giving the child a strong message that we are interested in what they have to say, that we take them seriously and that we will not be annoyed or upset by what they say will offer the encouragement that the child might need to say more. Depending on our role, there are different ways to gather more information. The most important message is to ask open questions. In investigative interviewing with children a particular command is used in questioning children about sexual abuse concerns: 'Tell me about that.' This avoids the danger of leading the child in the conversation. Apart from social workers and police, the role of the helper is to observe and record, rather than to ask questions about the concern itself. Being open to the possibility that abuse has occurred must be matched equally with being open to the possibility that there is another explanation for the child's distress. The key attitude is to keep an open mind. This way we will not miss the signals, nor will we jump to the wrong conclusion.

## Facilitating action

Each child is unique and needs a different response. Nevertheless, by taking some action in response to our concerns about children, we are giving them a strong message that we care and we are prepared to do something about their situation. When we notice changes in behaviour or mood in children, it is important that we do something. What that something is may depend on the child, on our relationship with the child, and the context in which we have contact with them. We may want to alert the child's parents to our observations or we may simply want the child to know that we have noticed. This in itself may provide the child with the opportunity that they need to come and talk to us at another time. We may need to create a private and safe place for the child so that we can encourage them to have a conversation. This again may help the child gain trust in us. They may not tell us right now what is bothering them but our action may speak volumes to the child: *I am here for you. I will listen to you. I will do something to help you.*

We can make suggestions as to how to make things better. If a child is having psychosomatic difficulties, we can think about ways to give them some extra attention or think of activities that we know they will enjoy. Psychosomatic communication is a cry for help – it is the only way the child can communicate their distress right now. We need to be able to hear the communication, even if we do not understand it, and help them find a way to communicate their distress in a way that we do understand. We need to help them take charge of themselves in a healthy way, by helping them manage their distress. By responding to their cry for help, we let them know that we are open to what it is they are trying to communicate, and that we will help.

Helplines can be useful to children in this regard – reliable and accurate information can be easily accessible, young people find this medium non-stigmatizing and they can maintain anonymity if this is what they need at this point in time, they have control over the contact (when it begins and when it ends) and they can use this support for a range of areas in their lives.

# Key messages

- Children often communicate their distress through their behaviour, their mood or through psychosomatic difficulties.

- Notice changes – changes in mood, changes in behaviour and signals that something is not right – and consider different possibilities as to what these changes might mean.

- Be aware of our own blind spots – our own biases, reactions and experiences and how these impact on how we listen to and notice changes in children's behaviour or mood.

- Draw children's attention to these changes – give the message that we notice and that we care.

- Invite a child to continue a conversation by using the phrase 'Tell me about that.' We may need to give children the language to talk about their feelings.

- Record our observations to help build up a picture over time. This helps us stand back and evaluate our concerns.

- Act on the communication we receive – by responding with action, we can help a child believe that they will be listened to and that we will do something to help them.

- Empower children and young people to recognize abusive situations in order to help them be aware of what constitutes abuse but also to engage them in conversations about issues such as consent and human rights.

# CHAPTER 6

# Asking Questions

Recent research has shown that most children disclose following prompts of some sort – where an opportunity is provided for them, by adults, to talk about what is happening to them. This can take the form of being asked directly if they have been abused in the context of concerning behaviour or comments on the part of the child. It may be a child care worker noticing that a younger child is masturbating repeatedly or an older child is repeatedly avoiding contact with a family member and behaving in a strange way when they are around. Opportunities such as these can help a child who has been abused to tell someone what is going on. It provides a reason to talk about a topic when there are few opportunities in their daily life to do so.

We now know that disclosure, like most sexual abuse, is a process rather than an event. Children typically say a little bit at a time, gauging the adult's response to their initial disclosures. Asking children about sexual abuse gives them the message that we are open to hearing their disclosure if and when they are ready to disclose. Children can also be provided with an opportunity to tell through questions being asked of them about their psychological wellbeing. This may be when a teacher notices that a child has been out of sorts for weeks on end and decides to take action by asking them if there is anything worrying them that they need to talk about. This may not lead to a direct disclosure in itself but it may pave the way for the child to make a direct disclosure some time later, either to the same person or to someone else that they trust. We have a responsibility to create opportunities for children to tell of their experiences. Asking children questions about their general wellbeing provides such an opportunity. Children need professional helpers to be 'vigilant': 'to have adults notice when things are troubling them'.[1] Asking a child questions about their general mood or behaviour can give them an opportunity to talk about what's on their mind. It can be extended as an invitation to chat, showing that we are interested in them, that we have noticed the change in them and that we are concerned for them. This may be just the message that they need to hear in order to feel that they can trust you enough to confide in you something they are struggling to articulate.

When we ask children about how they are and why they may be upset, we need to ensure that we ourselves are comfortable with having these kinds of conversations. We need to be prepared for the possibility that when we invite children to have a conversation, we may not like what we hear. We may be shocked and confused and not know what to do next. We may regret that they chose us to confide in. We need to be well prepared for these conversations, be able to contain the conversation in the event that the child discloses something of a sexual nature and know what to do next. This chapter describes children's experiences when they were asked questions that led to them disclosing and offers suggestions for helpers as to how we can help children tell.

We have learned a lot in recent years about how best to ask children questions when we are concerned that they have been sexually abused. Below, I will draw on research that has been carried out in the field of forensic interviews – where children are interviewed using a particular protocol or guideline when there are concerns that the child may have been sexually abused.

Helpers may be better placed than family members to facilitate disclosures. They are outside the situation and so they don't have the same vested interest in keeping the secret. As so much of sexual abuse occurs within families or the family's social networks, children are often conscious of the fallout of disclosure – how upsetting it may be for the parents and what is going to happen to the abuser. Having a distance can help. Sometimes it is easier for the child to talk about this with a helper whom they do not see on a daily basis.

---

1   HM Government (2013), p.10.

# What the research says

Research in recent years is continually showing us that when children do disclose this is often in response to questions being asked. In other words, the disclosure is elicited rather than offered spontaneously. In Chapter 3 I referred to various studies that highlight the dialogical or interpersonal nature of the disclosure experience. Children need opportunities to talk about what is going on in their lives. They need privacy to encourage them to talk about what may be difficult to describe and they need support from adults in having these conversations. They rely on the feedback they receive at each attempt to disclose in deciding whether they will share more information or tell more people.

In a study of interviews with 12–18-year-olds about their online activity,[2] young people spoke of how adults could help them by being observant of their activities, engaging them more in conversations about this activity and asking them questions about their activity, thus providing opportunities for such conversations.

## Many children tell when directly asked if they have been abused

We are aware from large-scale studies of both adults and adolescents that a significant percentage of respondents disclose experiences of childhood abuse that they have never told anyone before the survey (see Chapter 3 for details). In recent years, with the emergence of more qualitative studies of this phenomenon involving interviews with children and young people, we have come to understand better how often children's disclosures follow questions being asked of them, as opposed to them coming to us and purposefully telling us about their experience of abuse.[3] Children also describe being asked questions about themselves that appear to have helped them tell someone else a short time later. An example of this is a 17-year-old

---

2  Quayle *et al.* (2012).
3  Hershkowitz *et al.* (2007); Ungar *et al.* (2009a); Cossar *et al.* (2013); McElvaney *et al.* (2014); McElvaney and Culhane (2015).

girl who described how she didn't exactly tell her counsellor but she hinted that something was wrong:

> I didn't tell her what happened but I was saying things that made her think. It made her think that it happened but I didn't tell her.[4]

The following week, when another adult asked her what was wrong, she disclosed.

When children are asked directly, it is usually when someone has witnessed the abuse or observed some behaviour that makes them suspect that sexual abuse has occurred. One father noticed how quiet it was upstairs where he knew his son and an older nephew were playing. He went upstairs and found them in the bathroom. His son's trousers were down. A school teacher noticed children behaving in a sexualized manner in the school and asked them directly about this behaviour. This led to further disclosures of one of these children having been abused at home.

When children get older and form intimate relationships, this can be a trigger for being asked why they react in different ways. Some young people in my study described their friends or boyfriends asking them if they had been abused because of the way they reacted to certain jokes or because they seemed depressed. Rianach (aged 15) was one such young person who described how her parents or friends 'just knew by me...the way I was acting that there was something wrong'. Aoife (aged 18) described watching a TV programme with her mother about sexual abuse. Her mother reacted strongly to the programme. However, she also noticed how Aoife reacted. Aoife recalls how her mother 'knew by me face like there was something up' and asked her if anything like that had happened to her.

## Asking children about their distress is giving them an opportunity to tell

Adults typically question children when they notice signs that something is not right. Often this is manifested in the child's

---

4    McElvaney *et al.* (2014).

distress. Asking children about their distress is in itself giving them an opportunity to tell.[5] The most common way that young people in Cossar and colleagues' interview study came to the attention of services was through distress that was noticed by a professional or family member.

In my own research, I have suggested that asking children about their wellbeing can contribute to the 'pressure cooker effect' that is part of the process of disclosing for many children. It may be that by being asked questions about their mood and their behaviour, we can pave the way for the young person to tell the next time they are asked about why they are getting upset. Many of the children and adults I have interviewed describe a build-up of pressure to tell. One of the pressures they describe is when people ask them about themselves, such as asking: 'What is wrong?'

Eilis (aged 18) described her friend's observations when she was in the presence of the person who was abusing her:

> She was asking me, she kept on asking me, 'Are you okay?' I said, 'Yes I'm fine', and she was like, 'Are you okay?' … She kind of said something about the way the brother looks at me, 'What is he doing to you?' … She was the kind of person that would see through you…she just, she just kind of knew. I dunno how, but she knew.

This young girl only disclosed when a professional asked her directly. Even then, she could only write about it rather than say the words.

A young person in Cossar and colleagues' study kept an experience of rape to herself for a year, and was then helped to tell by a teacher. The young person attended a meeting where she was asked how she had been. The teacher was also in attendance.

> I was upset that past week and she asked me how I had been since the one before and I said I had been fine, and Miss said: 'Well that is not completely true because the last week has been not so good as it could have been.' And then I just started crying and she asked what was wrong and I said that

5 Kogan (2004); Collings *et al.* (2005); Jensen *et al.* (2005); Hershkowitz *et al.* (2007); Ungar *et al.* (2009a); Schaeffer *et al.* (2011); McElvaney *et al.* (2014).

I couldn't tell her. Then everyone else went and she stayed and she said: 'You can always tell me anything, because you normally do, so whenever you are ready just go for it.'[6]

The young person then showed the teacher her diary where she had written about the experience.

## Children can feel that they should have been asked

Some of the young people I interviewed said that they should have been asked directly if they had been abused. This would have made it easier for them to tell. Deirdre (aged 18) said:

I was waiting for her to say to me: 'Look has this happened?'

Deirdre described feeling resentful that her mother didn't guess what was wrong:

Mams just know things. I was kinda hoping that she would guess.

However, she did acknowledge that she might not have told her mother:

I don't think I would've said, yeah, but I think I would have made it quite obvious that that's what woulda happened.

Bronagh (aged 15) felt her grandmother should have known there was something wrong with her:

the way I was going on an' all cos I really wasn't meself... She shoulda guessed that there was something wrong with me.

Sometimes young people think that they are communicating to their parents that something is up but their parents are not picking up the signals. Parents can often put their behaviour down to their

---

6   Cossar *et al.* (2013), p.70.

being teenagers and don't ask too many questions, perhaps fearful of being rebuffed or aggravating their teenage children even further. As Cara (aged 15) put it:

> I kinda thought she knew even though I hadn't told her. Like I knew I hadn't told her, but I thought she would have figured it out.

Interestingly, in my study, some young people thought that the reason they were asked these questions was because the adult already knew that they were being abused. As I had the opportunity to interview parents as well as young people, I found that this was not the case. The adults did not suspect anything to do with sexual abuse. They just knew that something was wrong and they were concerned about their son or daughter.

Debbie Allnock and Pam Miller[7] found that many of the young people in their study either delayed their disclosure or did not tell at all because no one asked or noticed that they were in distress. Young people described a litany of missed opportunities whereby professionals did not ask them directly if something was wrong, thus denying them the opportunity to tell. They said they would have liked to have been asked directly about abuse and this would have helped them tell. They described how some professionals, such as teachers, noticed that something was wrong but appeared to be reluctant to get involved, or how social workers who were already engaged with the family about mental health issues didn't ask in a sensitive manner what was underlying these problems. They felt that more could have been done if professionals had taken the trouble to ask the right questions or look beyond the surface. Parents or neighbours later admitted that they had concerns but didn't act on them. The young people described feeling that professionals such as police, social workers, teachers and health care workers saw them as the problem.

Even when children are asked, they may not be ready to tell. Some of the young people I interviewed noted that children will not tell until they are ready. Bronagh (aged 15) said that it would depend

---

7  Allnock and Miller (2013).

on who asked her. For instance, she would have told her mother but would not have told a teacher. Many authors have discussed how children weigh up the pros and cons of disclosing.[8] There is therefore a reasoning process that takes place for many children, particularly older children, about whether on balance it is better to tell. In addition, emotional readiness – being prepared for the consequences, not knowing what will happen – is an important factor for children who come to tell. In my research, young people noted that when adults or friends did ask what was wrong, this contributed to the pathway to disclosure and to the pressure to tell.

## Sometimes children deny even when they are asked directly

We know from research on investigative interviews that a proportion of children who are interviewed in such contexts by professionals specially trained in interviewing children about sexual abuse concerns will deny that they have been abused when there is corroborative evidence to prove that they have been. The average disclosure rate across studies of children with gonorrhea was 43 per cent.[9] Another study of police interviews with children[10] found that children denied being abused even when there was videotaped evidence of the abuse.

## We can get it wrong in the way we ask children about abuse

Sometimes the protocols we have to follow when we are concerned that a child is being abused do not facilitate the young person being able to tell us about it. A young person in my research study spoke of being brought to see a social worker following an initial disclosure. Her mother's partner, who had abused her, was sitting outside the room while the social worker spoke with her. At this point she had not indicated who had abused her, just that she had been abused. She felt she couldn't speak about him when he was so close by. The

8    Bussey and Grimbeek (1995); McElvaney *et al.* (2014).
9    Lyon (2007).
10   Sjöberg and Lindblad (2002).

investigation led nowhere and the girl didn't tell again for another five years. Child abuse enquiry reports abound with examples of situations where professionals question children in front of parents who are later discovered to have been abusing their children or are in other ways unsupportive of any action taken to intervene. Professionals need to be open to the possibility that the parent or carer may be the perpetrator of abuse and not expect children to speak openly in their presence.

Young people in Allnock and Miller's[11] study described the investigations of their disclosures as being poorly managed, resulting in retracted disclosures or leading to the investigation being dropped. Young people described how on occasions teachers approached a parent about a disclosure in a context where one of the parents was the abuser or there was an issue of domestic violence in the home and the parent was unable to protect the child. Children were interviewed in a room with their parents, where at least one of the parents was the abuser. Young people expressed frustration at how teachers may believe their parents were supportive when they were not. They described how teachers might be relieved after discussing the issue with a parent, thus absolving themselves of the anxiety but leaving the young person unprotected. Sometimes this situation led to retractions. Young people also described social workers visiting the home and interviewing the child in the presence of their parent, providing no safe place for the child to talk. There were several examples of professionals investigating concerns within families – domestic violence and mental health – whereby professionals only spoke to parents and did not create an opportunity to speak to the young person alone. Young people interpreted this as professionals not being interested in them.

## Minding myself

Helpers are understandably concerned about asking children questions about sexual abuse. There is so much at stake when an allegation of sexual abuse is made. Helpers in their determination

---

11 Allnock and Miller (2013).

to do no harm by asking the wrong questions may do more harm by not asking questions at all. Given the criminal nature of this behaviour, there is always the possibility that there will be legal proceedings. Helpers can be reluctant to get involved in situations where they may be relied on at a later stage to give evidence about their conversations with children. They can feel anxious and de-skilled, lacking confidence in their own abilities and fearful of being pressurized to perform outside the parameters of their competence. It is therefore important to reflect here on what we can do to help children tell, what questions we can ask them and how, and ways we can mind ourselves in the process.

Professionals are wary about asking children about whether they have had experiences of sexual abuse. Children (and indeed adults) are suggestible. We are influenced in what we say and believe by the questions we are asked. Understandably, helpers are concerned that by raising the topic of sexual abuse they may be 'leading' the child to say things that are not true. We are aware from research in laboratory settings that it is possible for children (and indeed adults) to report seeing things they did not see and deny seeing things that they did. Much of this research when applied to the field of child sexual abuse has focused on questioning styles when interviewing children. There is a substantial body of literature on this subject that I could not do justice to in these pages.

However, what is important to discuss here is the anxiety that this research has created in professionals about asking children questions about child abuse. Because we know it is possible to influence a child's response by the way we ask the question, we can become frozen in our anxiety and instead of learning more about what ways we should be questioning children, we can play it safe and avoid asking any questions at all. What I argue here is that this avoidance will leave children at risk. We therefore have to find out how to do this in such a way that we do not unwittingly interfere with the child's story and overly influence what they tell us. However, we need to be able to talk about our own anxieties first.

In minding ourselves, *we need to be aware of and be able to talk about our anxieties in asking children questions.* This may arise from a concern that we will ask the question in the wrong way and overly influence the child's response. This is a valid concern and worth paying attention to. The anxiety may also arise from not wanting to hear about the unpleasant details that the child may tell us. A third source for this anxiety may be that we do not know what to do if the child does tell us something that will require further action. What do we say to the child? Who do we speak to next?

People have been wrongly accused of child abuse, sometimes because professional helpers have asked children questions in an inappropriate way that has led to incorrect conclusions. The child abuse 'scandals' of the past have cast a shadow over professionals' practice, so much so that in some cases professionals are too frightened to ask questions about sexual abuse out of fear that they are 'leading' the child.

*We need to become more comfortable talking with children about sexual matters.* In Ireland, a recent evaluation of the implementation of a relationships and sexuality education programme in secondary level schools highlighted discomfort on the part of teachers in discussing sexuality in the classroom.[12] The shame and embarrassment that children feel about the abuse experience and that significantly impedes their ability to disclose this experience can also be experienced by helpers. Many of us may feel embarrassed discussing sexual matters. We may believe that this is not a subject we should discuss with children – that they are too young for such conversations. Yet children are abused from a very young age and not having such conversations leaves them unprotected.

*We need to know the guidelines.* It is important to be aware of and to follow whatever guidelines are available in the workplace or organization where we are working with children. Professionals will have their own guidelines from either their employer or their professional body. It is important to be aware of these and know how to follow them. In each organization there will be a designated person who is responsible for ensuring that employees are aware of the procedures for reporting a child abuse or neglect concern. If in doubt, ask. It is always a good idea to contact a local social worker to ask advice if a helper doesn't know what to do next. If a social

---

12 Mayock, Kitching and Morgan (2007).

worker isn't available or there isn't anyone to go to, a call to the local police station may be the best option.

# How to help

When children are sexually abused, it impacts on their ability to *trust* others. Yet trusting in others is fundamental to being able to confide experiences of abuse. Children's difficulties in trusting can be compounded through their experiences of helpers, when they may have felt misunderstood or overlooked. How we as helpers engage with children and how we help them to build trust in us is fundamental to all our interactions with children and young people and has been shown in study after study to be a significant facilitator for children when they disclose sexual abuse. Children need trusting relationships in order to help them tell. As one young person in Cossar and colleagues'[13] study said:

> As I got to know her, then I started to trust her and things like that, and then I started talking to her. It is now a lot easier to tell her my problems.

## Facilitating awareness

Children and young people will drop hints and it is important that we listen to these hints and follow our instincts at times to ask more questions when we hear or notice them. In the SAVI study in Ireland, 88 per cent of participants noted that their parents had not discussed sexual abuse with them as children, but over half of the participants who were themselves parents had discussed it with their children.[14] Teachers and professionals who have regular contact with children outside the home are well placed both to observe changes in young people's mood and to ask young people general questions about their wellbeing when such changes are noted. Professionals need to be able to ask young people appropriate questions that enquire after

---

13  Cossar *et al.* (2013), p.75.
14  McGee *et al.* (2002).

their wellbeing, thus giving them the opportunity to disclose, and be able to respond to disclosures in such a way that children's need for containment is met.

Children need help to talk when things are bothering them. As helpers we can provide this help by creating opportunities on a regular basis where we ask children questions about their psychological wellbeing, thus creating an atmosphere and an expectation that these are things we are open to talking with them about. As one young person in Cossar and colleagues' study said:

> I find it hard to open up about things like that…but [youth worker] learned me.[15]

## Facilitating expression/taking action

Facilitating expression is a way of taking action. In asking children questions, we are taking action. Being able to ask children the right kind of questions when there are concerns about sexual abuse is linked to what we discussed in Chapter 4. If we are not open to believing what the child may have to tell us, this will influence how we talk with children and what kinds of questions we ask. We can ask questions that in fact discourage them from telling us. An everyday example of this is, in response to observing a child's reluctance to engage in play with other children, a helper asks: 'There's nothing wrong is there?' It is much easier for a child to respond 'No' to this question than to respond 'Well actually, there is.' The question conveys a message that 'I'm assuming there is nothing wrong.' This makes it more difficult for the child to talk about something that might be wrong. Another way of asking a question would be to ask a general question, such as 'Are you okay?' This gives the child the option to deny that anything is wrong if they are not able to talk about it, but also gives them the message that you have noticed something. A final option, which is somewhat more direct, is 'What's wrong?' It is fair to assume in this situation that something *is* wrong. This assumption is based on the observation that the child appears reluctant to engage in group play. The helper may be wrong of course

15  Cossar *et al.* (2013), p.113.

– there may not be anything 'wrong' from the child's perspective; or if there is something bothering them, it may be nothing to do with the group of children. Nevertheless, it opens up an opportunity for the child to be able to speak if something is the matter.

Research has shown that the kinds of questions we ask influence the level and accuracy of detail that children will provide in response to such questions.

Examples of questions we could ask are:

- 'Is there anything you want to talk about?'
- 'I notice that you've been very quiet lately. Is there something bothering you? Do you want to talk about it?'
- 'You seemed upset when we talked about that. Are you okay? Does it upset you to talk about that?'

After we have commented on what we have observed, and given an open invitation to talk, we might ask:

- 'What was the fight about?'
- 'Why did you do that?'
- 'Why do you not want to go there?'
- 'Why do you not want to go with the others?'

We can be accused of being nosy, but that's better than being accused of not caring. Cumulatively, these questions can help children to tell.

If a child begins the conversation by saying something vague that is not clear, a useful prompt is: 'Tell me more about that.' This prompt is used a lot in investigative interviewing, and research has shown that using this prompt generally elicits more detailed responses from children and more accurate responses.[16] What we are trying to do is to elicit as much information as possible that is spontaneously offered by the child.

If a child does indicate that something has happened, a good open question is simply: 'What happened?' And a good follow-on from this question is: 'How did that happen?'[17]

---

16  Lamb *et al.* (2008).
17  Ahern, Stolzenberg and Lyon (2015).

# Key messages

- Ask children questions about their distress – this can help them along the pathway of telling.

- Respond to children sensitively and effectively – this makes them feel safe, that they can trust us and that we know what we are doing.

- Tolerate not knowing – children can test the waters and may not be ready to tell until they feel safe enough to do so.

- When having conversations with children:

  - establish rapport in the conversation – help the child feel comfortable in the conversation

  - ask open questions

  - follow this up with: 'Tell me more about that'

  - write down what the child has said as soon as possible, using the child's own words.

# CHAPTER 7

# Understanding Self-Blame and Shame

Unfortunately, a persistent experience for children who have been sexually abused is that of them blaming themselves for the abuse or feeling ashamed of what happened to the point that this impedes their ability to tell someone else about it. Understanding how children think about the experience and why it is they blame themselves can help carers reassure children in ways that they need reassurance. Children mostly know that it is wrong and this makes them feel guilty. They feel they should have done something to stop it or prevent it from happening. The experience of abuse can be humiliating. Feelings of shame are very painful and so children may go to great lengths to avoid having to feel these painful emotions. Keeping the secret of sexual abuse is one way of avoiding feeling this shame.

Adults' responses to children's disclosure can contribute to children's self-blame and can prevent them from sharing more details or from fully disclosing if they sense that they are going to be blamed for what happened. In particular, our own childhood experiences can get in the way of our ability to be there for children. In this chapter I discuss how childhood experiences, in particular the experience of being abused, can impact on how we as helpers respond to children when there is a concern about sexual abuse. It is important, therefore, for helpers to mind themselves – for us to reflect on our own experiences and how these may have impacted on us. We need to be clear in our own minds as to where the responsibility lies when a child is sexually abused and to tailor our responses to what the child needs at that point in time. Reassuring the child that they are right to tell, that adults will take responsibility for what happens now and that the child is not in any way to blame for what happened will help alleviate their fears about the perceived consequences of disclosure and their experiences of shame.

As human beings we tend to believe, rightly or wrongly, that we have a sense of agency – that is, control over our lives – and that we are responsible to some extent for what happens to us. This is a normal part of child development – to believe that we are the centre of the world, that the world revolves around us, that we are omnipotent and can control the world around us. This is referred to as 'egocentricity' and is important for the development of our sense of self. This normal part of child development may go some way to explaining why many children believe that when they are abused it is somehow their fault. Children who observe their parents fighting often question whether they are to blame. They refer everything that happens in their world back to themselves. When something happens that is out of our control, it impacts on our sense of ourselves as people who can manage ourselves and our lives. It can 'take the rug from under us'. It can undermine our sense of agency – we can feel helpless, hopeless and lose our belief in ourselves. We can all relate to this – revisiting an experience over and over to see what we could have done differently (the 'if onlys'). Inherent in this way of thinking is a belief that we are somehow responsible for what happened. This is a major difficulty in the area of sexual assault and rape, where, even in the most unlikely circumstances, women and men blame themselves for being assaulted. This can be difficult for others to understand and empathize with – it seems so illogical since it is clear to the listener that the person was in no way to blame for the assault or the abuse.

It can be even more difficult for adults to see that children, too, blame themselves. Somehow, we think that because children are so innocent and helpless they wouldn't think that they are responsible for bad things happening to them. So we can overlook the fact that children blame themselves.

Abusers often capitalize on the egocentricity of children and their tendency to shoulder the blame for what happens to them. In their attempt to absolve themselves of their responsibility for their behaviour, abusers can say things or behave towards the child in a way that leads the child to blame themselves for the abuse.

Sometimes the shame or self-blame comes from *messages that children received* from significant adults in their lives – comments such as 'You're useless' or 'Can't you ever get it right?' Children internalize these messages and as they grow older they no longer need anyone to give them these negative messages – they have internalized this voice that tells them that they're useless and can't get anything right. When something bad happens to them, it strengthens this inner voice and makes it even more difficult for the child to challenge it.

Self-blame can be the child's *way of coping*, of psychologically surviving the experience – they blame themselves rather than a parent or loved one who abuses them. This can be difficult for others to understand, but for psychological survival it is easier for us to blame ourselves than to blame someone we love. If we blame them, we experience a huge loss that can be very painful. To avoid this pain, we blame ourselves. For the most part, children love their parents and they want to protect them, even at a very early age. When their parents do something wrong, part of this protective instinct is to take on some responsibility for what the parents did. Alice Miller describes how the child must at all costs protect their belief that their parents are good – even to the extent that the child will see themselves as bad rather than see their parent as bad. This is a psychological survival strategy so that the child can maintain some sense of stability and control over their world. To face up to the reality – that their parent has done something bad, and so in the child's eye, is bad – is too psychologically threatening for the child.

When a child feels ashamed they want to hide and not be seen; they want to withdraw from social contacts. There is a sense of not wanting to show themselves and an accompanying belief that 'if they really knew me they wouldn't like me', or often, 'if they really knew what happened to me they wouldn't like me – they would be disgusted/revolted/find me repulsive'. As I discussed in Chapter 2 when describing the psychological impact of abuse, children can believe they are fundamentally flawed because something bad happened to them.

When children blame themselves for what happened, this can engender a sense of shame, the feeling that *they have done something wrong and feel ashamed about it.* Shame can be associated with self-blame but it can also stem from other sources. Children who suffer from low self-esteem can often feel shame as a result of feeling unloved and unlovable. We know that children with low self-esteem are both more vulnerable to being abused and more vulnerable to developing psychological difficulties as a result of abuse. Poor self-esteem is also associated with shame.

All child abuse can impact on the child's sense of self, engendering shame, but sexual abuse is particularly shame-inducing because of the *stigma* and disgust associated with sexually abusive behaviours. Children often feel disgusted when they think about the abuse, and this disgust is often turned on the self – because the abuse is disgusting, the belief is 'I am disgusting'. Children and adults describe feeling dirty. Victims of rape describe having a shower and scrubbing and scrubbing themselves in the belief that somehow the sexual assault has made them filthy and if they can scrub away 'the dirt' they can obliterate in some way what happened to them. Unfortunately, in the absence of being able to talk about the experiences, this shame goes unchallenged. Children may engage in self-harming behaviour or aggressive acting-out behaviour, which in itself perpetuates their feelings of shame.

The day will never come when it is not a shameful thing to be sexually abused. One might argue that this is only right because sexual abuse is wrong; it is shameful behaviour and we should never forget that. However, when children are engaged in shameful behaviour, this makes the child feel ashamed and that is unfortunate. It would be very interesting to compare those children who felt very ashamed as a result of being sexually abused and those who didn't. In my experience, the children who do not feel ashamed are those who have a good sense of themselves, are clear that the abuser was at fault for what happened, are not in a close relationship with the abuser, were able to tell someone immediately after it happened, and were believed and protected.

## What the research says

Many children feel ashamed about the experience of sexual abuse and feel embarrassed about it due to the sexual nature of the experience. Shame and embarrassment have been described as some of the most common reasons for children delaying or not telling about their experiences of sexual abuse.[1] Younger children, under around seven years of age, tend to be less likely to talk about feeling shame or embarrassment as this experience is linked to the development of self-consciousness.[2]

Feeling responsible for the abuse has been found to be a significant predictor of delayed disclosures.[3] As one 18-year-old girl I interviewed put it:

> When you're like about 12 and you don't have anybody to talk to and you don't know what actually happened…you do start believing that it was your fault, so you don't tell anybody… I started believing like that it was my fault, then it wasn't even about the threat anymore, it was about because I thought it was my fault so why would I tell somebody, why would I tell somebody something that it was my fault that I did it.

Abusers often deliberately set the child up to feel that they have some say in what is happening – for example: '[H]e said that I was bad that's why this is happening.'[4] Abusers sometimes even believe this themselves.

The self-blame may arise from the child's inaction or not fighting back – pretending it wasn't happening is a common coping strategy for children.

> I was awake like, but I didn't turn around and say here like 'Stop!' I didn't push his hand away, you know that kinda way.[5]

---

1   Kellogg and Huston (1995).
2   Saywitz, Esplin and Romanoff (2007).
3   Goodman-Brown et al. (2003).
4   McElvaney (2015b), p.177.
5   McElvaney (2015b), p.176.

In the absence of an explanation as to why it was happening, some children blame themselves:

Is it my fault, is it? Why did it happen?[6]

People are more likely to blame older children than they are younger children,[7] suggesting that older children are perceived as more responsible for the abuse. One adult I interviewed spoke about telling her adult children about her experience of sexual abuse when she was nine – but she didn't tell them about the experience she had when she was 12 as she felt more ashamed of this incident and felt more responsibility for 'allowing it to happen'.

When children disclose at an earlier age, they are given the opportunity to be told that it was not their fault. The extent to which self-blame develops as a direct result of keeping the secret is an interesting question to explore. In the absence of being able to tell anyone about it, thoughts of *self-blame can develop over time*.

> I think that as I got older I started to think... I couldn't think of any reason why would he do that to me like I musta done something or I must just be a certain type of person, d'ya know what I mean?... It was just like I did question when it first happened. I was thinking, 'Well is it my fault or isn't it?', but then I started believing that it was my fault.[8]

An adult I interviewed described how in therapy she reflected on the experience and questioned how she didn't stop it:

> I allowed that to happen... I obviously allowed it to happen. Why wasn't I strong enough? Why, why didn't I shout? Like, I mean there was seven of us there...in one bedroom...so he just had to creep in when everybody was sleeping, you know, why pick me, you know? You know afterwards when you're talking to [therapist] or whoever about abuse, you know it just occurs and you think to yourself, you know, why did I allow that to happen, you know?

6    McElvaney (2015b), p.177.
7    Waterman and Foss-Goodman (1984).
8    McElvaney (2015b), p.177.

Sometimes when there is no physical coercion, this can lead to a sense of self-blame – 'Well I didn't try to stop it, did I? or 'I wasn't forced, was I?'

Unfortunately, because children who have experienced abuse are at higher risk of being victimized later, feelings of self-blame can get perpetuated if the child is victimized again.

> I just didn't want anyone to know. I was so angry with myself, ashamed with myself that it would happen again.[9]

When children do tell, they can feel responsible for the fallout from their disclosure. Children feel responsible for the family breaking up, for people being removed from the home, for children not being able to see their parent. One young girl I interviewed retracted her disclosure because of the guilty feelings she had when her little sisters missed their Daddy and couldn't understand why he couldn't live with them anymore. From an adult's perspective:

> I mean, you say to yourself: 'God why did I not, eh, run out of the room when he opened the door... Why could I not say to me Ma, "Now Ma, I don't want this, this man here. He's, eh, messing around with me."' ... I really, I musta been really thick... It's always that shame that you feel, God, I coulda stopped that you know?[10]

Another source of self-blame is when the child felt sexually aroused by the abuse – when their body reacted to the stimulation in a pleasurable way. This is extremely confusing for children. As they grow older, it can become more shameful as the developing adolescent or young adult comes to understand more about sexual arousal and asks themselves the question: 'Did I enjoy it? How could that be? Does that make me a horrible person?'

Sometimes it is through therapy in adulthood that people come to realize it was not their fault, by meeting others in similar situations.

---

9   McElvaney (2105b), p.176.
10  McElvaney (2015b), p.178.

It's like there was only two years in the difference and that's when you start thinking, 'Well, he was only young himself'... At one stage he did pin me down and then after that it wasn't, it was just taken kind of a thing, that's where I woulda been ashamed of is the fact that I had let him because I had no choice... You know 'em, it's my fault, so what's the point in saying anything? ... I think when you're told, then okay, yeah, he came into my room so that's where your brain, your brain is starting to say, 'Well, I wasn't, I didn't go into his room', and start making you realize, then, 'Oh God, maybe is that my fault?' ... You know that he was the one that approached my room, I didn't approach his room.[11]

Some children are able to arrive there themselves:

When I started to really think about it, I just realised like it wasn't my fault. I was scared I didn't do anything wrong.[12]

Young adults in Allnock and Miller's[13] study spoke of their feelings of shame, embarrassment and guilt and their need to be spoken to sensitively but directly. The authors highlight the importance of ensuring that conversations take place in a private location, respecting young people's need for privacy.

Not all children and young people believe that the abuse is their fault. One young person in my study noted that she never thought it was her fault. Her parents had separated when she was younger and they had always reassured her that it wasn't her fault. This seems to have helped her when she was struggling with the experience of abuse. She didn't tell, but not because she thought it was her fault.

## Minding myself

Listening to children's stories about sexual abuse can be very difficult. We can feel disgusted that someone can do such a thing to a child.

---

11  McElvaney (2015b), p.178.
12  McElvaney (2015b), p.177.
13  Allnock and Miller (2013).

We can want to recoil from the experience of listening – not wanting to hear what is being said and not wanting to imagine it. It can be traumatic for the helper to be exposed vicariously to what a child has experienced. I recall an experience many years ago where as a young and inexperienced psychologist I viewed videos of men abusing children. The videos had been found in the house of someone who had just been arrested and there was concern that some of the children who featured in the videos might be local children who would need help. Afterwards, I felt I shouldn't have just sat there and watched them as I felt increasingly uncomfortable sitting in a room with two strangers watching this material. I got flashbacks of the images over the months following this experience.

As helpers, we can experience the psychological impact of the trauma 'by proxy'.[14] This is referred to in the literature as *vicarious traumatization' (VT)*. Listening to the difficult material can be distressing. Too much exposure to this material can lead to difficulties similar to those experienced by those who have had direct exposure to the trauma: intrusive thoughts or images about the experience, a tendency to avoid situations, people or places that remind us of the experience, or a hypersensitivity or hypervigilance that manifests itself as anxiety. It is a similar concept to compassion fatigue, whereby a helper may lose the ability to empathize with another as a result of repeated exposure to people who experience trauma. VT refers to when the helper's world view is altered fundamentally as a result of exposure to other people's trauma. The helper develops negative belief systems about issues such as safety, power and their sense of self. They may become distrustful of themselves and of others, thus impacting on their social, family or intimate relationships. They may become suspicious of others and experience mood difficulties such as depression and anxiety. They may experience emotional numbing or avoiding places or people that remind them of the traumatic material. Alternatively, they may experience feeling overwhelmed or be flooded with emotions about the child's experience. Ironically, it

---

14  McCann and Pearlman (1990); Pearlman and Saakvitne (1995).

is through our ability to be there for others, to empathize with them and to 'feel their pain', that we are vulnerable to developing VT.

The literature has identified some contributing factors that make some of us more at risk of developing VT than others. Those of us who have a trauma history of our own are more vulnerable. Some research suggests that inexperienced helpers are more vulnerable (because they have not yet developed effective coping strategies), while others suggest that more experienced helpers (because of the cumulative impact) are more vulnerable. Other factors may be emotional style (some people are more sensitive to others' emotional states), coping style (some people are better at managing and regulating their emotional reactions) and individual circumstances (other stressors in people's lives, along with what supports people have). The need for confidentiality can make it difficult to find opportunities to debrief or rely on the supports that we usually rely on in other parts of our lives. This can lead to us feeling isolated and unsupported.

There are a number of protective coping strategies to help us avoid VT:

- Having someone to talk to in order to 'offload' and reflect on concerns and try to make sense of the situation.

- Being well tuned into ourselves, acknowledging how we feel and how we react, and recognizing our limits and our coping resources. An awareness of trauma – knowing how it can affect people – is important.

- Maintaining a good balance, both personally and professionally. Personal coping strategies can include keeping good boundaries between work and home life – it helps not to think about work when we are at home.

- Nourishing our relationships – spending time with people we like and having fun – helps to nourish ourselves.

- Those who have a strong faith base may find comfort in religious beliefs and rituals. Others may express their spirituality in different ways – through meditation, art or other creative outlets.

• Finally, good physical nurturing of the self is important, through diet and exercise.

# How to help

## Facilitating awareness

The natural reaction for us all when it comes to shame is to avoid: to avoid feeling the shame, to avoid thinking about it and most of all to avoid talking about it. The helper may need to steer the conversation in that direction, respecting the child's need and right not to talk but at the same time helping the child face up to their difficult feelings. This is a difficult task and best undertaken when we have a good relationship with a child. We need to be able to recognize when the child is avoiding facing up to their feelings and when they are simply not able to engage in the conversation right now.

We can educate children and help them understand that it is never okay for an adult to hurt a child in this way, and that it is *always* the adult's fault when this happens. Children can be taught this as part of general education in keeping themselves safe. We can also use other life experiences to illustrate to children that adults' behaviour is their responsibility. One 15-year-old girl I interviewed described how she had never thought the abuse by her mother's partner was her fault:

I always knew it wasn't my fault because everybody said that. I always had that drummed into me: 'It's not your fault'... See, when my parents broke up, people always said, 'It's not your fault, we're just not getting on, it's nothing to do with you', and when (alleged abuser) and Mum had rows, Mum always said, 'It's not your fault'... So, no, I always knew it wasn't my fault.

The language we use is important as the way we say things conveys as strong a message to a child as the words we use to say it. For example, when faced with a child who looks guilty, as if they have done something wrong, adults can make the mistake of asking 'What did you do?' This reinforces the child's belief that they did something, rather than that something was done to them. Children do not understand how easily adults can coerce them into behaving in a certain way and they do not see how manipulative adults can be with them. They think they are a lot more powerful than they are, so it is difficult for them to understand that they had little power in a situation where they had been groomed and coerced into a sexually abusive interaction or relationship. We need to counteract this belief by constantly reinforcing the message that children are not to blame for bad things that happen to them.

## Facilitating expression

It is important that we respond to children by reinforcing the importance of talking about their experiences, particularly when they feel ashamed about them. Talking about shameful experiences can dilute the intensity of the shame. It gives the child the opportunity to be responded to in a caring, supportive way and to challenge their belief that if they tell people about this, they will be rejected or shunned. Helping children express the negative feelings they are having, putting into words their negative self-statements helps to mediate how these statements are undermining the child's self-esteem. Children need reassurance that it is good to talk and that telling is the right thing to do. When we let children know that we understand – for example, by saying, 'It must be hard to say that' – this helps the child feel heard and understood, and encourages them to talk more about their experiences.

It can be very difficult for children to accept that what happened was not their fault. It is therefore necessary to help them articulate why they think they were to blame. Perhaps they were given sweets by this person or treated in a special way and they liked this. Then it's important to acknowledge that of course if someone gives you sweets and is nice to you, you think they are a nice person. If they kept going back to visit a person who sexually abused them, they can believe that in going back again and again they were active participants in the sexual abuse. Then it's important to validate the part of their behaviour that involved going back – of course if you like someone and they are nice to you, you will go and visit them again and again. We need to help them separate out the 'nice behaviour' from the sexual abuse behaviour. Going back to visit someone does not mean that the child wanted to be abused again. That does not make the sexual abuse their fault.

It is difficult for us to challenge children's beliefs about their experiences if we do not know what they are thinking. Children are such creative beings that it can be difficult for us to second guess them when it comes to wondering what sense they are making of their experiences. It is important not to assume that we know how children have been affected by their experiences of abuse – we need to give them space to tell us what they are thinking and feeling. Helping them express their feelings and articulate their thoughts and beliefs helps us to understand how they are doing and gives us the opportunity to challenge unhelpful beliefs that may be reinforcing their feelings of shame and self-blame. Sometimes it's helpful for us to tell children how others might feel in this situation, being careful all the time not to assume that this is how it is for them.

Some children find it hard to talk about what happened because it's embarrassing to talk about sex at all, never mind something sexual that has happened to them. It's important to use the child's words as far as possible. Sometimes, children don't have the language to talk about sexual abuse, or sexual matters in general and they may need some help with this. However, there is always a danger when talking with children about sexual abuse that as adults we interpret what they are saying and make assumptions that we know what they are talking about when perhaps we don't. The safest path in this instance is to stay with the words the child has used, while encouraging them to talk further. An example of this would be if a child described being touched on her 'jina' by her uncle's 'willy' and 'it was sore'. You may know as a result of a child abuse investigation that the child has disclosed penile–vaginal penetration. It may be important for the child that you continue to use her words – 'touch', 'jina' and 'willy' – when you are helping her talk about how she feels about this and how she is trying to make sense of it. It's important to reassure her that it was a very bold thing to do for her uncle to touch her jina with his willy.

## Facilitating action

Helping a child to voice their negative thoughts helps them to become more aware of the automatic thoughts that they have and to realize how self-destructive these thoughts and the accompanying feelings are. It also makes these thoughts more accessible so they can be challenged. Understanding the child's self-statements also assists the helper in identifying what it is the child really needs (to be loved, to be understood?). The child needs to be helped to access more positive self-statements and to understand that what happened to them was wrong, that someone else is at fault and that they deserve to be treated better. Helping children to find opportunities for standing up for themselves in their daily lives can help them deal with shame since it reinforces for them the belief that they are entitled to be treated with respect and thus supports the development of their self-esteem.

Providing a 'corrective emotional experience' for the child through a caring and reassuring response helps the child to develop their sense of self: getting positive feedback that they are a good person in some way addresses their shame.

## Key messages

- Children often feel that when bad things happen, it is their fault and they often blame themselves for being sexually abused. This is not necessarily 'logical' – it just *is*.

- As helpers we can be impacted by listening to children's stories about their experiences. We need to make sure that our own reactions do not contribute to children's feelings of shame and self-blame.

- We need to be careful about how we speak with children – children can be very sensitive to interpreting what we say as blaming them further.

- Children need to receive constant and persistent messages:

  - It was not your fault – it was his/her fault.

  - Children are never to blame for being abused.

  - It is okay to talk about what happened – talking helps.

  - It's good to stand up for yourself – you deserve to be treated with respect.

# CHAPTER 8

# Helping Friends to Tell

*Significant proportions of adolescents disclose to their peers before telling an adult.* How these peers respond to such disclosures is crucial for the psychological wellbeing of both the young person who discloses and the young person to whom the disclosure is made. This chapter addresses how we as helpers can both facilitate this adaptive behaviour and at the same time support young people through the process to ensure that they get the help they need.

Some years ago, a barrister told me a story of a young girl who confided in her friend that she was being abused. Her friend 'marched' her down to the local police station and insisted that she report the abuse. While this may not work for everyone, it was a very clear, no-nonsense response, which resulted in the successful prosecution of the abuser. The barrister commented to me: 'We must be doing something right.'

Educating adolescents about sexual abuse would therefore appear to be a crucial target in any prevention programme that aims to encourage early disclosure of child sexual abuse. How peers respond to such confidences may rely on their own awareness of the issue and their accessibility to a trusted adult. While more research is needed, my own studies have suggested that in some cases, friends have been an important link in the pathway to disclosing to child protection authorities or police. However, in other cases, telling a friend may have relieved the emotional pressure for a while, resulting in prolonging the secret-keeping process. While young people can be an important resource for prevention, in order to avoid overburdening them it is important that they are supported in how they support others. As one young person in Cossar and colleagues'[1] study said:

> I think it's too much responsibility, for someone to be able to…like, if someone had come up to me, I wouldn't know what to do, where to go, not straight away anyway. If they're, like, 'Don't tell anyone, don't tell anyone', I wouldn't know what to do. I'd be really confused and that would be too much responsibility.

If we can educate young people about what to do if their friend discloses sexual abuse, and encourage them to seek support from an adult or a professional helper, we may be able to intervene sooner, preventing ongoing abuse and helping young people to get the support they need.

This phenomenon of young people disclosing to friends first is more typical in adolescence but is also a feature of pre-adolescent children. There isn't a clear pattern emerging from prevalence studies as to whether children are more vulnerable to sexual abuse before the teenage years, but there is some evidence to suggest this. McGee and colleagues found that most of the adults in their studies who reported experiences of abuse in childhood had these experiences before the age of 12 (67% of girls and 62% of boys).[2]

## What the research says
### Having good quality friendships is a protective factor for young people who experience difficulties

Much has been written about the developmental advantage of friendships for children, the psychological benefits of friendships (or 'chumships' as the psychoanalyst Harry Stack Sullivan called them) and how friendships could mediate the psychological impact of negative life experiences. Psychological outcomes for young

---

1   Cossar *et al.* (2013), p.91.
2   McGee *et al.* (2002).

people can vary depending on having friends or not, who one's friends are (socially competent or antisocial) and the perceived quality of friendships (for example, supportiveness).[3] Positive peer relationships are a protective factor for young people when dealing with adversity. Young people who enjoy strong friendships are less likely to experience anxiety and depression,[4] tend to have better self-esteem, tend to suffer less from anxiety and have better overall psychological wellbeing.[5] The reciprocal impact of friendships is important, particularly for children with internalizing difficulties – isolation in peer relationships can result from sadness and depressed affect as the child withdraws from the social group, and the isolation can contribute to poor mental health when there is conflict or exclusion.[6]

We know from research in developmental psychology that peers promote emotional security and good social skills. They also encourage the young person to engage with and explore their environment and can be particularly beneficial for vulnerable young people. In general, female–female peer relationships tend to facilitate more intimate disclosure than male–male peer relationships.[7] Peer relationships become even more important when relationships to parents or caregivers break down. Friends provide emotional protection and compensate for the lack of emotional resources available to vulnerable young people from their families.[8]

Positive peer relationships help promote better mental health and education outcomes.[9] The social support that young people receive from each other helps their self-esteem and provides opportunities for developing interpersonal skills in how to relate and to manage relationships, particularly ruptures in relationships. Being part of a supportive peer group protects children and young people from being targeted for bullying or other negative experiences. Also, being liked by our peers is both an important experience for developing our

---

3   Hartup (1999).
4   La Greca and Harrison (2005); Bukowski, Laursen and Hoza (2010).
5   Buhrmester (1990).
6   Bukowski *et al.* (2010).
7   Buhrmester and Furman (1987).
8   Sanders *et al.* (2014).
9   Ladd (2005).

sense of ourselves as good and likeable human beings and protects us from the negative impact of not being liked by others.

Studies that have specifically examined the role of friendships in how children cope with the impact of sexual abuse have underscored the role of friends. Satisfaction with friendship relationships has been shown to be associated with children's self-worth and to have helped with the impact of abuse,[10] while an absence of friends compromises psychosocial wellbeing.[11]

## A significant proportion of young people tell friends first

We know from the research that younger children are more likely to tell parents, while older children are more likely to first confide in a peer. There is also some suggestion from research that adolescence may be a 'critical period' for disclosure, regardless of when the abuse occurred.

A study of calls to ChildLine Scotland found that young people aged 12–14 years were twice as likely to tell a friend as a parent.[12] A US study of adolescents showed that those aged 7–13 were more likely to tell an adult, while those aged 14–17 were more likely to confide in a peer. The most common initial confidante was a close friend (36%).[13] Peers have been found to be the most popular choice of first confidante in several studies of adolescents.[14]

Friends are often the first to notice that something is wrong, even when they don't know – or even suspect – about abuse. They are often someone that young people trust to keep the information confidential until they are ready to talk to an adult, and they provide emotional support through the disclosure process and the aftermath of disclosure.[15] In a review of studies of adults who were abused in

10  Feiring, Taska and Lewis (1998).
11  Sanders et al. (2014).
12  Vincent and Daniel (2004).
13  Kogan (2004).
14  Crisma et al. (2004); Schönbucher et al. (2012).
15  Allnock and Miller (2013).

childhood, when adults told someone as a school-age child 'the most common confidant was another adolescent'.[16]

Sometimes adolescents turn to their peers rather than adults because of difficulties trusting what adults will do with this information. Many young people have spoken of the need to keep control over the process of disclosure and they fear that this control will be taken from them when they tell an adult. Adolescents also fear that if parents find out about the abuse they will curtail their freedom by placing restrictions on their movements in an unwanted effort to protect them. While there is much written about how young people turn to peer relationships when parent–child relationships are poor,[17] most of the young people in my study had a positive relationship with their parents, which in itself was a barrier to disclosure as they were anxious not to upset their parents.

Young people are also more likely to confide in their peers than in adults about unwanted experiences with other peers.[18] Thus, the nature of the abuse experience also influences whether young people will tell peers or adults first.

## Friendships provide a context for disclosing when confidences are being shared

Sean (aged 16) said:

> We were talking about our problems, em, [boy] was talking about how he was feeling suicidal…and [girl] was telling us her problems. Like she has an eating disorder and, em, we were trying to help her with that and then, like out of nowhere, like, I just felt like saying it.

Some of the young people I interviewed described how their *friends helped them tell an adult.* The boyfriend of Maire (aged 16) persistently encouraged her to tell her parents over a period of two years. When she did first tell her father, she just told him some of

---

16  London *et al.* (2007), p.201.
17  Barber and Olsen (1997).
18  Kogan (2004); Sperry and Gilbert (2005).

the story. Her boyfriend insisted that she tell her father everything that had happened.

A friend of Caitlin (aged 14) also persisted:

> She just kept on nagging me: 'Do tell tell your Mam, it's the right thing to do.'

A friend of Blathnaid (aged 17) pointed out the risks to other children if she didn't tell:

> What if he goes and does it again, like, why don't you? You just be the one to deal with it now.

Friends of Dympna (aged 16) told her not to continue to babysit for her sister, whose partner was abusing her, and to tell her parents. She described how this helped her to realize the seriousness of what was happening and why it was important to tell:

> The more they told me and explained and, you know, told me how big a deal this [is], I think it helped because the more you understand how bad it is and you know the whole situation of there's children involved and you know…and I think the easier it is for you to tell cos you're giving yourself more reason.

Young people are sometimes cautious about telling their friends about abuse – they choose carefully who they tell and who they don't tell, based on whether they can trust the friend not to tell others.[19] Interestingly, some young people describe the benefits of not telling friends when they want to be able to forget about the abuse and get on with their day-to-day lives. Others do not want to worry their friends – they are concerned about the impact that knowing about the abuse would have on their friends.

---

19  Cossar *et al.* (2013).

## Friends provide support and help young people tell

With the increasing use of the internet among young people as a way to communicate with their peers, this has become a useful way to investigate young people's views in a more anonymous way. Jeanette Cossar and her colleagues analyzed data from an online forum where young people were invited to post threads about experiences of abuse and neglect and help-seeking. This study offers us some understanding of how peers offer each other support in a virtual environment. The postings were anonymous. The online forum provided an opportunity for young people to communicate directly with other young people who had similar experiences. The types of support offered by peers in 251 posts was as follows: 88 per cent (220) offered emotional support that consisted of sympathy, empathy or encouragement; 69 per cent (172) encouraged the young person to tell an adult; 48 per cent (121) provided suggestions to help the young person understand why it was happening or ways to think about the situation differently; 36 per cent (91) disclosed that they too had similar experiences; 35 per cent (87) offered suggestions as to what the young person could do next, apart from telling; and 26 per cent (66) offered ongoing support in the form of committing to respond to future posts.

Some of the responses were seen as helping the young person recognize the behaviour as abuse or neglect and therefore had an educational component, targeted at facilitating awareness. Others focused not on whether it was abuse or not but on giving a clear message that it was wrong and therefore an adult should be told about it:

> No matter what you call it, it's wrong. If it makes you feel so bad that you self-harm, then you definitely need to talk to someone about it.[20]

Most of the responses acknowledged the difficulties in telling. Some gave advice as to how to make it easier, such as writing notes to

---

20 Cossar *et al.* (2013), p.50.

people or practising telling before doing it in reality. One young person gave detailed advice:

> Start by saying that something is happening that you don't like. If you are still finding it hard to say what it is, you could ask them to ask you questions and you answer yes and no… [A]t some point they will probably need you to actually say it and give names. When it came to that, I asked the person I was telling if they could turn and face another direction and not look at me when I said it.[21]

## Friends are not always supportive

Young people can also have negative experiences of telling friends, such as being teased, called names, being isolated or being treated differently.

> All the girls keep hugging me and saying: 'It'll all be alright and if I need to talk, they're always there.' I know they're just being good friends but it is so patronizing. And they're making it sound like I have some kind of disease or something… The boys say stuff to me like: 'Have you ever kissed anyone, I mean apart from your stepdad?'[22]

Some of the responses in Cossar and colleagues' study encouraged the young person to confront the person who was hurting them in the belief that they would change their behaviour. Some young people gave advice as to how the young person should change their own behaviour, implying that they were doing something wrong and needed to change. The dangers of social media were also highlighted as on occasion young people posted messages about a friend's experience of sexual abuse, thus informing a large group of young people about something without checking out with their friend whether they were comfortable with people knowing about it.

---

21  Cossar *et al.* (2013), p.51.
22  Cossar *et al.* (2013), p.49.

## Disclosing to friends may also mean that young people don't tell an adult

Depending on what happens next, I have suggested that confiding in a friend can relieve the 'pressure cooker effect' for young people. Now they have shared their secret, the burden doesn't feel so heavy. They have someone to talk to, which to some extent eases their psychological pain. This can result in the secret being contained for an additional period of time, until the pressure builds up again and the young person needs to tell an adult. Young people I interviewed described keeping the secret within a peer group for up to five years. A US study of adolescents[23] found that the likelihood of revictimization was four times higher for those young people who did not disclose to an adult. Many of the young people in this study who experienced revictimization had disclosed to a friend.

# How to help

As helpers, we can educate young people about friendship relationships – both healthy and unhealthy ones. Helping young people develop healthy friendships protects them from the risk of being targeted in unhealthy relationships. We can help them learn how to respect each other, to understand the importance of trying to see things from others' perspectives, how to manage ruptures in relationships in a healthy way and how to support each other in a way that is helpful to all. Finally, we can be there for them when they need to turn to an adult.

## Facilitating awareness

Many children are engaged in a process of grooming as a prelude to being sexually abused. Being able to recognize when grooming is happening is very difficult for young people and indeed for families and other adults. Grooming is deceptive and manipulative, which is why it is such a successful mechanism used by abusers to draw

---

23 Kogan (2004).

children into complying with inappropriate sexual behaviour. Part of the deception is the abuser being nice, kind or generous – behaviour that can be authentic. It can be extremely difficult to detect abusive behaviour that appears to the observer to be benevolent. Grooming can also result in cutting children off from supportive adults in their environment, as the abuser becomes a support person for the child.

Young people need to be taught that when an adult takes a special interest in a young person, this can be an example of grooming. Young people are particularly well placed to notice when a friend is receiving special attention from an adult – when they are given lots of attention, gifts such as toys, money and computer games. A young person may be more inclined to confide in a friend than an adult that they have an older teenager or adult as a 'special friend'. It can be difficult for a child or young person to give this up – they may sense that if they tell someone about it, they might lose this special friendship. It is important, therefore, to understand what the child or young person might be gaining from this relationship. It may be that they are in need of support at this time, that they are experiencing a difficult time at home or in peer relationships. It is important for young people to understand that even when we have good resources in terms of coping with difficulties in our lives, when we are going through a bad patch those resources are depleted. We are not as well able to cope as when things are going well. Children may need extra support at that time and are particularly vulnerable to being lured into inappropriate relationships at times of strife.

According to many authors, approximately one-third of sexual abusers in the United States are adolescents. Added to this is the relatively recent phenomenon of sexualized behaviour among children whereby children are coercing each other into engaging in sexual behaviour that can range from mildly intrusive, such as 'I'll show you mine if you show me yours' to attempted and actual digital, vaginal or anal penetration with very young children. Children therefore need to be taught *to protect themselves from other children*. Teaching children about healthy relationships involves teaching them how to stand up for themselves in peer relationships when they are asked to do something they don't like, that they think is wrong, or that simply makes them feel uncomfortable. The grooming behaviour described earlier that adults engage in to recruit children into sexually abusive behaviour is also evident in children whereby children are especially friendly, give gifts or money or special favours and show preferential treatment of one child over another in peer groups as a means of deceiving the child into believing that they are a special friend, only to be the victim of intrusive sexual behaviour that can be very difficult for a child to tell an adult about.

## Facilitating expression

Engaging young people in conversations about what helps young people tell, how to facilitate such conversations and how to help others express themselves fosters awareness and encourages expression. We can provide opportunities for children and young people to discuss peer relationships – What makes a good friend? When is a friend not being a good friend? We can ask young people about their views on how to manage difficulties in peer relationships, thus encouraging them to talk about this, to share their views and to develop their own coping strategies in these relationships. We can explore with them what to do in various scenarios and encourage them to come to us to talk about these struggles, thus establishing relationships and expectations that it is okay to speak with an adult about these difficulties.

## Facilitating action

Young people are a wealthy resource for us as helpers in knowing how to help them to help themselves. We can encourage young people to talk to each other, to engage in fun activities both as a means of getting pleasure and as a means of distraction when needed. We can encourage them to get involved in activities together – physical activities or other activities that help to enhance the young person's sense of belonging in their peer group. We can teach young people how to provide emotional support and in so doing to look after themselves. Some of the ideas from Cossar and colleagues' website analysis[24] include:

- Keep busy.
- Keep active to help with sleep.
- Flick a wrist band to prevent self-harm.
- Avoid situations where the abuse is taking place.
- Make sure other people are around to prevent opportunities for the abuse to take place.

In my own study, young people talked about feeling understood by their friends, their friends 'being there' for them. The emotional support was invaluable to them in navigating their way along the pathway of disclosure.

## Key messages

- Children and young people, particularly in the teenage years, are more likely to first confide in a friend rather than in an adult.

- It can be more difficult for children and young people to disclose peer abuse to an adult than to another young person.

- Young people need increased awareness about healthy relationships – what is okay and what is not okay – so that they can recognize when someone is behaving towards them in an inappropriate way.

- Young people need to know what to do if a friend confides in them that they have been abused. In particular, they need to know to approach an adult to help them with this.

---

24 Cossar *et al.* (2013).

CHAPTER 9

# After First Disclosure

This chapter will discuss research on children's experiences following disclosure and highlight the types of support that children need following such disclosure. Supporting children through this process is challenging, particularly when helpers themselves may feel disheartened and frustrated by the wider systemic response to the child's disclosure. The helper's own doubts about the value of disclosing may need to be addressed, in order to support the child and family through the aftermath of disclosure. In addition, the process of disclosure is an ongoing process through the lifespan – decisions regarding disclosure will be made again and again in new relationships and in new contexts. This chapter will also draw on interviews with adults about their experiences of disclosing in adulthood, how the delay in disclosing impacted on them, and their reflections on advice they would offer to children today.

As discussed in Chapter 1, there are three goals for us as helpers in dealing with the aftermath of disclosure, which are:

- to prevent further risk of sexual abuse or sexual victimization, to the child concerned and to other children
- to mediate the psychological impact of the abuse
- to prevent secondary trauma that may result from the consequences of disclosure – fallout in the family and engaging with the legal system.

We know that the relationship between disclosing the abuse and mental health symptoms is mediated by the response of parents and significant others.[1] A negative response is associated with mental health difficulties while a positive response is associated with better coping abilities and more positive mental health outcomes. How we respond to children when they disclose is therefore crucial in working towards good outcomes for children who have been abused.

Some children experience relief when they disclose. The burden is lifted, or at least shared. Difficulties that were experienced prior to disclosure may abate. Children may be able to sleep better and they may present in better mood. Some children may need to talk about it, while others may not find this helpful. Each child is unique and needs a unique response. The best advice is therefore to know the individual child and tailor our responses to their individual needs. It is by observing and monitoring children that we get a sense of what they need and what is best for them at any given time.

While it may be a relief for some, for others it may be very scary. Keeping the secret has been for them a way of managing the situation. Disclosing the secret relinquishes control to others. They know that there will be consequences. Action will be taken. There will be upset and there will be trouble for the person who abused them. This responsibility that children feel for others is a heavy burden but not one that is easy to relinquish. They need a lot of reassurance that everything is going to be okay. There can be much uncertainty as to what will happen now and it is challenging to provide children with reassurance when as professionals we do not know what will happen. This is why it is important to communicate to children what we do know and what we can be sure about. We may not know what will happen in the longer term but we probably do know what the next step is. Keeping children informed from one step to the next is one way of providing reassurance and helping them to cope with the uncertainty and unpredictability that is a key feature of child abuse investigations. Sometimes, too many services get involved and leave the child feeling out of control:

> I just felt better that I had told someone, but since then
> it has just got a bit harder and harder... It just got harder

---

1    O'Leary *et al.* (2010).

because there are so many appointments and people that I have got to see.[2]

Sometimes children regret that they have told. There may be breakdowns in family relationships following the disclosure. Parents may be very distressed. Children and families have to engage with systems that they may not have had any prior experience of: the child protection system and the police. Children may be continually asked questions about what happened. It may all seem too much and children may feel they would have been better off if they had kept the secret to themselves and not told and that, somehow, the stress of coping with the secret was easier than the stress of coping with the consequences of disclosure.

Sometimes families try to contain the issue within the family and not go to the authorities. Less is known about these situations unless the issue is eventually brought to the attention of the authorities. Nevertheless, we can empathize with parents who think they are doing the best thing by trying to contain things. Understandably, they may be reluctant to go to the authorities when the abuse is by a family member. There is more motivation to believe that this may have been a 'one-off' incident, that it isn't serious and that it is just a matter of making sure the child is not left alone with the abuser. They may be reluctant to confront the abuser if this person is a mother's or father's brother or sister. They may be anxious not to cause a fallout in the extended family – for example, they may feel they need to protect an elderly grandparent from the truth of what their son or daughter has done. Such families may be difficult to engage with, and as helpers we may find it very challenging: to try to help where help is not wanted.

Some children will need professional counselling or psychotherapy. It is important not to assume that all children need professional help. Many children will be able to cope with the aftermath of abuse by relying on their own psychological resources and the support they get from families, friends and other helpers. Other children may appear to need professional counselling but not want to engage with it; they may not want to talk about their experiences and believe

---

2   Cossar *et al.* (2013), p.81.

that forgetting about it is the best way to move on. The children and young people in Cossar and colleagues' study[3] saw school as a place where services were accessible, and where children saw helpers every day and had an opportunity to build up a relationship. Children described how having support workers based in the school made it so much easier to approach them to talk whenever they needed to. Youth workers were also identified as important professionals who supported young people in the aftermath of disclosure.

For many children and young people, the psychological impact of the abuse is felt more after the abuse stops rather than during the experience of ongoing abuse. We can relate to this in terms of how we all cope with difficulties. At the time, we just need to focus on coping and getting through it. When it is over, sometimes we collapse and feel really upset about what happened. Sometimes, stopping the abuse can take on too much of a focus with not enough attention paid to the support needed by the child when the abuses stops.[4]

The criminal aspect of child sexual abuse brings children into contact with the legal process. As helpers, we need to be cognizant of the types of conversations we have with children following a disclosure; the possibility of legal action must always be kept in mind and also the potentially contaminating effect that our questions, our responses and our comments may have on the child's testimony. For this reason, the number of formal interviews undertaken with a child about concerns of sexual abuse is kept to a minimum. Procedures for investigating sexual abuse have both a civil and a criminal component. The civil aspect is the role of the statutory authority responsible for protecting children. Decisions will need to be made about protecting the child who has disclosed and possibly other children who have contact with the alleged abuser. The criminal aspect is the role of the police, who are responsible for preparing a file that can be used by the state for prosecution purposes. In helping children following disclosure, we need to be able to keep the balance between offering the child a safe place to talk about

---

3   Cossar *et al.* (2013).
4   Cossar *et al.* (2013).

whatever they need to talk about but remaining careful about what we say to children – we need to be supportive but not put words into children's mouths. We need to encourage children to talk about their experiences but be aware that we can influence their memories of events by comments we make or questions that we ask.

There is a long history of unreported sexual offences to the police authorities both by adults and by children. With increased awareness of the recidivist nature of sexual offending, more efforts have been made to prosecute offenders, leading to more focused investigations by the police. Practice varies in different countries as to how investigations are conducted, but increased co-operation between child protection authorities and law enforcement authorities has in many countries resulted in an increased rate of legal investigations. In my own research comparing adults adults' and adolescents' experiences,[5] just two of the ten adults I interviewed had any police involvement – in both cases as children. For one of these women, her first experience of sexual abuse had been reported as she had told her mother immediately and there was a police investigation that was later dropped, apparently at the request of her family. She was later abused by a different individual, but this time she didn't tell anyone. The memory of the police investigation and the turmoil in the family home at the time of the earlier investigation prevented her from telling. In the group of adolescents, 13 (65%) of the young people had experienced some form of police involvement. Many parents are reluctant to engage with the legal system in cases of sexual abuse. They are concerned about the impact that this will have on their child.

Many adults who have experienced sexual abuse in childhood have managed to cope with the impact of the abuse for many years without thinking much about it. They have found ways of coping, through perhaps not thinking about it and avoiding people or places that might remind them of the experience. For many, something happens in their life that brings the memory back into the foreground. People describe not being able to stop thinking about it, having flashbacks of the abuse itself and feeling anxious or depressed or

---

5   McElvaney (2015b).

irritable for no apparent reason. They may need professional help to be able to manage these feelings and the impact that they are having on relationships. They may not have told most of the people in their social network about the childhood experiences and find themselves faced with the dilemma of disclosing. Should they tell others to explain why it is they are not able to cope with life? What will people think? The stigma associated with sexual abuse leaves people feeling that they will be judged or blamed, that people will think of them perhaps in the way they think of themselves – as partly responsible for what happened. They may fear a loss of relationships, particularly if the person who abused them is a family member. People may not believe them, choosing instead to stand by the accused, questioning why, if this really happened, it wasn't said years ago?

## What the research says
### Fear of the consequences of disclosure

Studies have consistently shown that one of the reasons children do not disclose immediately following abuse is the fear of what will happen if they do. Goodman-Brown and colleagues[6] found that fear of consequences was a significant predictor of delayed disclosure in children in the United States who were seen in a district attorney's office. Other studies have shown that many of the fears children have about the consequences of disclosure are realistic fears.[7] Children are *not* believed. They *are* blamed – sometimes for the abuse, sometimes for telling. There *is* trouble – sometimes for themselves and their families, and always for the alleged abuser. Things *do* get worse. Families *do* break up. Sometimes things *do* get out of control for a bit. Reassuring children that their fears will not be realized is not always a good idea as children may then feel let down by the false promises they were given by professionals.

Unfortunately, difficult as it is to tell about sexual abuse, this is for many children just the beginning of a difficult process. We

---

6   Goodman-Brown *et al.* (2003).
7   Herskowitz *et al.* (2007); McElvaney *et al.* (2014).

know from studies of adults that many had negative experiences following disclosure that in themselves had a traumatic impact on the individuals involved.[8] Interestingly, Ullman's[9] study of college students described more negative experiences following disclosure as a child than as an adult. In my own research comparing adults' and adolescents' experiences of disclosure, more young people (85% – 17) than adults (50% – 5) believed that telling would make it worse.

> Like I thought it would've. If nobody knew about it, well then I'd still be like... I'd still be with me sister and the kids would be over and it wouldn't cause any pain for anybody, only myself. I'd feel bad coz he'd get in loads of trouble an' everything and then I was saying: 'God like this is much easier not to say anything.'[10]
>
> My life fell to pieces. I was mental no doubt about it...in my case 'Before' [at home in an abusive environment] was actually better than 'After'.[11]

Children may be afraid of retaliation from the abuser for having told:

> I'm scared he's going to kill me because I've broken my promise.[12]

They may need reassurance that they are safe now and that they will be protected.

Sometimes young people feel overwhelmed following disclosure and often they are worried about what will happen next. A common theme is young people feeling fearful of not being in control.[13]

Unfortunately, much of the research in this area focuses on the negative consequences of disclosure rather than on positive experiences. One young person in my study[14] suggested that helpers

---

8   Hunter (2011); Alaggia (2004); Jonzon and Lindblad (2004); McElvaney (2015b).
9   Ullman (2007).
10  McElvaney (2015b), p.184.
11  Cossar *et al.* (2013), p.48.
12  Cossar *et al.* (2013), p.48.
13  Ungar *et al.* (2009b).
14  McElvaney (2015b).

could get children thinking of possible positive outcomes for children when they disclose sexual abuse – stories of children telling and their life being better afterwards.

Nevertheless, we can learn from understanding more about these negative experiences. Young adults have spoken of what they found unhelpful in professionals following disclosure:[15]

- They did not like the way professionals spoke to them and they were not informed as to what would happen next.

- Some professionals focused more on the young people's difficulties, thus seeing the young person as a problem, rather than the abuse.

- They did not have enough support from professionals such as the police and social care professionals.

- There was no one-to-one support during the court process.

- Poor handling of follow-up disclosures resulted in retractions and negative reactions by family members to the disclosure.

- Sometimes files were closed and the young person was left not knowing why.

- Some felt that the professionals involved did not do their job properly in following up the disclosure.

The three key positive features of disclosure experiences described by these young adults were that:

- the person to whom they disclosed believed them
- they acted in response to the disclosure
- the young person received emotional support to help them cope with the aftermath of the disclosure.

This emotional support consisted of being believed, having someone they could trust to talk to about the abuse, and having support in making reports to authorities in the form of someone being with the young person when they made their report or providing moral support.

---

15  Allnock and Miller (2013).

Young people have said that the aspects of relationships with helpers that promote trust include the duration of the relationship, being believed by the professional, not being judged and closeness.[16] In addition, the perceived knowledge and expertise of the helping person was identified as helpful as well as the effectiveness of the support and the accessibility and availability of services. Young people talked about the importance of professionals not making assumptions about them or their distress, not judging them or jumping to conclusions and believing them. One young person described how a youth worker helped her because of her non-judgemental attitude:

> Like I kept feeling that I am a criminal, I have messed my life up, everything has gone wrong for me and whatever, and she [youth worker] just made me feel so much better. She was just like: 'You could turn it all around.'[17]

In my PhD research, I asked children and young people what advice they would give to helpers about helping children to tell. These are some of the responses:

- Ask.
- Give them time.
- More supervision.
- Just sitting down and talking to them.
- A helpline.
- You shouldn't give help when you're not asked.
- Go to a teacher, face to face you can't just hang up the phone.
- Don't make me do anything I don't want to do.
- If they see their child being down or something, do ask them, just let them know you can tell them something.
- Reminding children of things they said.

---

16 Cossar *et al.* (2013).
17 Cossar *et al.* (2013), p.75.

- Just keep on telling them it's not their fault.
- Make them feel safe.

## Children may want us to keep the secret

Children and young people place great emphasis on confidentiality – the need to keep the information confidential when they do disclose. Concerns about people not keeping the disclosure confidential can act as a barrier to telling:

> You don't open up to anyone unless you trust them and it takes a lot to build trust and then for you to get that trust and then act like you are not going to tell no one and then tell someone, that is disgusting... Don't ever think that I am going to trust you again.[18]

However, young people often understand and agree that in some circumstances it is right for professionals to pass on information without young people's consent:

> If it is something severe and incredibly serious, like sexual abuse or child abuse, then no matter what the child says it should be passed on.[19]

Young people need most of all to be kept informed about the limits of confidentiality and about when information needs to be passed on. Young people have described how this can in fact strengthen relationships with helpers rather than damage them when it showed that the helpers cared about them:

> Because she told me that she had done it, she was also worried about me, just knowing that she was like worried about me...it just made me feel like I could talk to her about pretty much anything.[20]

---

18  Cossar *et al.* (2013), p.76.
19  Cossar *et al.* (2013), p.76.
20  Cossar *et al.* (2013), p.78.

Young people wanted helpers to explain to them why, when and what information would be passed on, to listen to their views and concerns about this and to take account of how this might make their situation worse.

Young people in this study also acknowledged the burden that keeping the secret entails and that it is easier for the professional to do the reporting than it is for the child:

> And then I think that with a teacher they would do all the work for you, so then you don't have to sit there going: 'I want to talk to a social worker, I need to do this.' Do you know what I mean, they would help you and they would do it for you?[21]

Practitioners have also noted that many young people wanted the responsibility of keeping the secret to be taken from them, even though they might have asked for confidentiality. Young people might purposefully tell someone in authority because they want something done:

> Actually they do want you to tell, they do actually want you to take control, they are children and actually want an adult to lead them and an adult to do something about it. And if they perhaps justify this by saying 'but don't tell anybody', it absolves them of that responsibility.[22]

However, one important lesson from the research is the need for consistency among helpers. An example of inconsistency from Cossar and colleagues' study[23] was when one professional (a school nurse) kept the information confidential while another (a GP) passed the information onto social services.

---

21 Cossar *et al.* (2013), p.78.
22 Cossar *et al.* (2013), p.93.
23 Cossar *et al.* (2013).

## Young people need support following disclosure while awaiting legal hearings

Involvement in legal proceedings brings many challenges for children. Children may feel worse over time, having to cope with the anxiety about the hearing and lack of information about what is happening. Children have described feeling fearful of seeing the perpetrator in the courtroom and finding this difficult. One concern highlighted is how mental health professionals were more concerned with symptoms than being a support to the young people.

> I went to child psychiatric department but they did not think I needed any help because I was not suicidal. I would have needed to talk to someone professional.[24]

Helpers were not always helpful – one young person described a church support worker saying to her:

> It is your own fault. You blame others for the sexual activity, but you were not cautious yourself.[25]

Children talked about the need for support:

> It should have been more support around me even if I said no to it, so I did not understand what I needed. I could not understand myself what I could not cope.[26]

They also emphasized the need for just one professional to support them throughout the legal process – a professional who was competent and understood both the legal process and child sexual abuse.

## School can be a place of healing

Children spend a lot of their time in schools. Outside the home, teachers are often the adults who are best placed to notice when children are distressed or something is not right. Through their role as educators, teachers are well placed to educate children about their

---

24 Back *et al.* (2011), p.54.
25 Back *et al.* (2011), p.54.
26 Back *et al.* (2011), p.54.

rights and help them recognize when their rights are being infringed. Recognizing abuse as abuse can be incorporated into the curriculum, and opportunities for discussing issues such as the nature of sexual abuse and consent can be addressed in schools if teachers have the necessary support both personally and professionally to do this. As state employees they also have a child protection role and knowledge about the state system that parents often do not have. Research studies cite examples of where teachers did not act on information, leaving a child to stay in an abusive situation,[27] as well as examples of where the teacher did intervene, leading to the abuse being stopped and the child getting much-needed help.[28] Such studies refer to teachers not wanting to intrude into children's personal lives, suggesting that there may be some confusion for teachers in their role in child protection and mental health. In my own research,[29] children, parents and adults who experienced childhood abuse spoke of the importance of having someone available in schools that children can approach if they need to talk about sexual abuse. In some jurisdictions, school-based counselling is available and social workers are based in schools. In others, access to such services is much more difficult.

## Minding myself

The National Guidelines in Ireland for responding to child abuse concerns describe *working in child protection as working with uncertainty*. I think of the analogy of walking the tightrope. If we are too anxious, we lose our balance, children sense this from us and we undermine ourselves in what we are trying to achieve. We have to have all senses on alert and pay attention to not just the child in front of us but also our own response to the child, to our breathing, to how we are feeling and to what anxieties are being triggered, taking care not to dissuade the child from confiding in us. If we are too intense, we will lose them; if we are too cautious, we won't

---

27  Cossar *et al.* (2013).
28  Allnock and Miller (2013); McElvaney (2015b).
29  McElvaney (2015b).

get anywhere. We also have to pay attention to the wider context: we have a duty of care to the child to ensure that we act in their best interests. How to do this is often not clear. We need to think about the family, the child's schooling and other supports or lack of them. We have reporting obligations that will need to be addressed. We have our own fears and anxieties as to what will be the fallout, not just for the child and their family but also for ourselves. We are entering an arena that is fraught with uncertainty, blame and dire consequences for those who 'get it wrong'. These are real fears that need to be acknowledged. On the positive side, when on the receiving end of a disclosure, we are in a unique position to help this child. While the anxiety to get it right can be threatening to us, the opportunity to get it right can also be stimulating and rewarding. Many of us in the helping professions are drawn to this work for that very reason: we can really make a difference in this child's life.

What are the *concerns of the helper* after a child has disclosed? These can be that we will get it wrong, that we will damage the trust that the child has in us and that services will not follow through and the child's fears about disclosure will be realized – things will get worse. Sometimes the obligation for us to pass on information immediately, following the guidelines available, can place us in a difficult situation where we are concerned that, on the one hand, we leave ourselves open to criticism if we don't follow the guidelines, but, on the other hand, we may lose the relationship with the young person. We may scare them off and prevent them from being able to get the help they need. It is not just the loss of the relationships that concerns us; we may fear that we will do more harm by reporting the matter. Enquiries into child abuse and child deaths have left professionals feeling vulnerable and anxious – we are damned if we do, and damned if we don't. As helpers, we can overreact to situations out of anxiety that we will get it wrong, or that we will be leaving a child unprotected if we don't act immediately, when what we need to do is discuss it with a colleague, take time to reflect on the consequences of our behaviour and feel confident that we are taking the right action.

Our own *faith in the system* that responds to children following disclosure also impacts on how we respond to children. In countries where professionals are mandated to report concerns about sexual abuse to child protection services, one of the reasons for non-referral is the concern on the part of the professional that children would not be helped as a result of the report. Helpers are concerned that mishandling of child sexual abuse allegations will leave children more unprotected than before they disclosed. They are also concerned that children's negative experiences following disclosure will inhibit them from making future disclosures and will impact negatively on their self-esteem and self-efficacy, reinforcing their sense of self-blame.

*Professionals may fear being blamed if they do not act on information immediately.* Professionals describe concerns about not sharing information immediately in case they were blamed if something went wrong.[30] This can interfere with helpers being able to make good judgements as to how to respond to sensitive information such as this and what action will be in the best interests of the child. It is also important to take account of the child's family context – gathering information about the family and the likely consequences of disclosure – to help in making judgements about what to do next, keeping the child's welfare at the forefront of our minds.

# How to help
## Facilitating awareness

We can facilitate awareness for children and young people first through raising awareness about sexual abuse and how people react to disclosure and second through giving concrete information about the processes that the young person has to engage with following disclosure. It may be important to reassure children that other children have had these experiences, and it is in no way their fault that people are reacting in the way they are. We can help children by informing them of what may happen next. Children and families can experience considerable anxiety following disclosure, and not knowing what will happen next exacerbates this anxiety. We may need to make some enquiries ourselves as practice tends to vary in

---

30 Cossar *et al.* (2013).

different regions. There is often some degree of uncertainty as to what might happen next as more information may need to be gathered that will in turn inform these decisions. It is important not to make false promises as the breaking of a promise can be much more harmful to a child or young person than the anxiety created by uncertainty. If the helper does not know what will happen next, it is best to say so. Whatever certainty can be offered should be offered. Beyond that, it is best to be honest. Children are vulnerable at these times and need some certainty and predictability in their lives. What is important therefore, is that as much information as possible can be shared with them, but with caution in the event that decisions change.

## Facilitating expression

It is important for children to be able to talk about their fears and anxieties about what will happen and what is happening. They need to be able to say out loud what worries they have, such as whether the alleged abuser is going to punish them or others in some way, or that terrible things are now going to happen. They will need reassurance but most of all they need to be able to express these concerns.

Professionals responsible for the wellbeing of the child following disclosure are rightly cautious about having conversations with children about what happened. They are concerned that they may leave themselves open to accusations of leading the child or influencing the child in some way. As discussed in Chapter 6, the best advice to follow after disclosure is not to ask questions about the abuse itself but to confine questions to asking about the child's wellbeing. When the child talks about what happened, continue to show interest and, wherever possible, write down what the child has said. Focus on how the child is, how they are feeling and what thoughts they have. It is important for many children that they are able to talk about their thoughts and feelings. It is also important for them to get feedback about these thoughts. Children can blame themselves for co-operating in the abuse. They need reassurance that it is never a child's fault when an adult does something to them that makes them feel uncomfortable.

Keeping things general in this way, rather than focusing on the child's unique story, and reinforcing this message over and over, can be helpful. We can also tell the child that it is always a good thing to tell an adult when someone does something that is not right.

Concerns about the limits of confidentiality are best dealt with as an ongoing part of our work with young people. It is best to make it clear from the outset that we want to encourage them to tell us what is bothering them but there may be situations when we will have to tell someone else about this. A suggestion from one of the practitioners in Cossar and colleagues' study is:

> You can tell me anything and there are some things that you tell me I will have to share, if I feel that, you know, either you yourself or somebody else is in danger; I will have to share that information.[31]

## Facilitating action

As professional helpers, when we deal with a child, we are representing all professionals. If we provide them with a good enough experience in each interaction we have with them, we increase the likelihood that they will come back to us when they need to, or if not us then another helper. First and foremost we need to reassure children that telling was the right thing to do. Children will doubt that they should have told and they will be fearful of what will happen. They need to know that despite what happens next, it was right to tell.

It is important that the young person retains some sense of control and that their sense of agency is respected – they should be able to say what they need to say and choose when they wish to say it. Young people value adults' help because they take control and are effective but they also need to be kept informed of what to expect and to be forewarned when information needs to be passed on. While they do have a need to keep some control over the information, this is an inappropriate burden for the child to carry, which may leave them feeling more responsible not only for the abuse, but for keeping the secret and for protecting the abuser or protecting their family from the painful knowledge of what has happened.

---

31 Cossar *et al.* (2013), p.92.

It is sometimes necessary for helpers to mediate with parents during and after the first disclosure. Children need to be helped to express their fears and doubts about how they perceive and understand their parents' and others' reactions. It may be necessary to represent the child's voice to parents and to help parents understand the complex feelings and thoughts that children struggle with after they tell. Parents are going through a difficult time too, and they may need support in order to support their children. Children need to voice their concerns about others finding out – peers, extended family and neighbours – and to have these concerns taken seriously. They need to have a say in who knows and who doesn't know. They need to be listened to, and if a decision is taken that they don't agree with, it is important to explain why this decision is being made.

---

## Key messages

- Reassure children that telling was the right thing to do.

- Be aware that when dealing with parents, they may have undisclosed experiences of childhood sexual abuse and may need help themselves.

- Be aware of the system we work in – the policies and procedures.

- Be open and honest: things may become more difficult for a while.

- Don't 'catastrophize'. Children do overcome the psychological impact of abuse; some do not experience negative effects and some report psychological growth.

- Seek support to manage frustrations with the system.

# REFERENCES

Ahern, E. C., Stolzenberg, S. N. and Lyon, T. D. (2015) 'Do prosecutors use interview instructions or build rapport with child witnesses?' *Behavioral Sciences and the Law 33*(4), 476–492.

Alaggia, R. (2002) 'Balancing acts: Reconceptualizing support in maternal response to intra-familial child sexual abuse.' *Clinical Social Work Journal 30*(1), 41–56.

Alaggia, R. (2004) 'Many ways of telling: Expanding conceptualizations of child sexual abuse disclosure.' *Child Abuse and Neglect 28*(11), 1213–1227.

Alaggia, R. (2010) 'An ecological analysis of child sexual abuse disclosure: Considerations for child and adolescent mental health.' *Journal of the Canadian Academy of Child and Adolescent Psychiatry 19*(1), 32–39.

Alaggia, R., Michalski, J. H. and Vine, C. (1999) 'The use of peer support for parents and youth living with the trauma of child sexual abuse: An innovative approach.' *Journal of Child Sexual Abuse 8*(2), 57–75.

Allnock, D. and Miller, P. (2013) *No one noticed, no one heard: A study of disclosures of childhood abuse.* London: NSPCC. Available at www.nspcc.org.uk/services-and-resources/research-and-resources/2013/no-one-noticed-no-one-heard, accessed on 3 March 2016.

Angelou, M. (1984) *I Know Why the Caged Bird Sings.* London: Virago Press.

Back, C., Gustafsson, P. A., Larsson, I. and Berterö, C. (2011) 'Managing the legal proceedings: An interpretative phenomenological analysis of sexually abused children's experience with the legal process.' *Child Abuse and Neglect 35*(1), 50–57.

Bagley, C. and Young, L. (1987) 'Juvenile prostitution and child sexual abuse: A controlled study.' *Canadian Journal of Community Mental Health 6*(1), 5–26.

Barber, B. and Olsen, J. (1997) 'Socialization in context: Connection, regulation, and autonomy in the family, school, and neighbourhood, and with peers.' *Journal of Adolescent Research 12*(2), 287–315.

Barron, I. and Topping, K. (2010) 'School-based abuse prevention: Effect on disclosures.' *Journal of Family Violence 25*, 651–659.

Bentovim, A. (1992) *Trauma Organized Systems: Physical and Sexual Abuse in Families.* London: Karnac Books.

Briere, J. (1997) *Psychological Assessment of Posttraumatic States.* Washington: American Psychological Association.

Briere, J. and Elliott, D. M. (2003) 'Prevalence and psychological sequelae of self-reported childhood physical and sexual abuse in a general population sample of men and women.' *Child Abuse and Neglect 27*(10), 1205–1222.

Buhrmester, D. (1990) 'Intimacy of friendship, interpersonal competence, and adjustment during preadolescence and adolescence.' *Child Development 61*, 1101–1111.

Buhrmester, D. and Furman, W. (1987) 'The development of companionship and intimacy.' *Child Development 58*(4), 1101–1113.

Bukowski, W. M., Laursen, B. and Hoza, B. (2010) 'The snowball effect: Friendship moderates escalations in depressed affect among avoidant and excluded children.' *Development and Psychopathology 22*(4), 749–757.

Buljan Flander, G., Cosic, I. and Profaca, B. (2009) 'Exposure of children to sexual content on the internet in Croatia.' *Child Abuse and Neglect 33*(12), 849–856.

Bussey, K. and Grimbeek, E. J. (1995) 'Disclosure Processes: Issues for Child Sexual Abuse Victims.' In K. J. Rotenberg (ed.) *Disclosure Processses in Children and Adolescents*. New York, NY: Cambridge University Press.

Classen, C. C., Palesh, O. G. and Aggarwal, R. (2005) 'Sexual revictimization: A review of the empirical literature.' *Trauma, Violence, and Abuse 6*(2), 103–129.

Collings, S. J., Griffiths, S. and Kumalo, M. (2005) 'Patterns of disclosure in child sexual abuse.' *South African Journal of Psychology 35*(2), 270–285.

Collin-Vézina, D., Sablonni, D. L., Palmer, A. M. and Milne, L. (2015) 'A preliminary mapping of individual, relational, and social factors that impede disclosure of childhood sexual abuse.' *Child Abuse and Neglect 43*, 123–134.

Collishaw, S., Pickles, A., Messer, J., Rutter, M., Shearer, C. and Maughan, B. (2007) 'Resilience to adult psychopathology following childhood maltreatment: Evidence from a community sample.' *Child Abuse and Neglect 31*(3), 211–229.

Cossar, J., Brandon, M., Bailey, S., Belderson, P., Biggart, L. and Sharpe, D. (2013) *'It takes a lot to build trust' Recognition and Telling: Developing earlier routes to help for children and young people*. London: Office of the Children's Commissioner.

Council of Europe (2012) *Council of Europe Strategy for the Rights of the Child (2012–2015)*. Available at www.coe.int/t/DGHL/STANDARDSETTING/CDcj/StrategyCME.pdf, accessed on 3 March 2016.

Crisma, M., Bascelli, E., Paci, D. and Romito, P. (2004) 'Adolescents who experienced sexual abuse: Fears, needs and impediments to disclosure.' *Child Abuse and Neglect 28*(10), 1035–1048.

Cross, T. P., Walsh, W. A., Simone, M. and Jones, L. M. (2003) 'Prosecution of child: A meta-analysis of rates of criminal justice decisions.' *Trauma, Violence and Abuse 4*(4), 323–340.

Department of Children and Youth Affairs (2011) *Children First: National Guidance for the Protection and Welfare of Children*. Dublin: Department of Children and Youth Affairs.

Dooley, B. and Fitzgerald, A. (2012) *My World Survey: National Study of Youth Mental Health in Ireland*. Dublin: Headstrong.

Dube, S. R., Anda, R. F., Whitfield, C. L., Brown, D. W. *et al.* (2005) 'Long-term consequences of childhood sexual abuse by gender of victim.' *American Journal of Preventive Medicine 28*(5), 430–438.

Easton, S. D. (2012) 'Disclosure of child sexual abuse among adult male survivors.' *Clinical Social Work Journal 12*, 1–12.

Easton, S. D., Coohey, C., Rhodes, A. M. and Moorthy, M. V. (2013) 'Posttraumatic growth among men with histories of child sexual abuse.' *Child Maltreatment 18*(4) 211–220.

Elliott, A. N. and Carnes, C. N. (2001) 'Reactions of nonoffending parents to the sexual abuse of their child: A review of the literature.' *Child Maltreatment 6*(4), 314–331.

Feiring, C., Taska, L. S. and Lewis, M. (1998) 'Social support and children's and adolescents' adaptation to sexual abuse.' *Journal of Interpersonal Violence 13*, 240–260.

Finkelhor, D. (1994) 'The international epidemiology of child sexual abuse.' *Child Abuse and Neglect 18*(5), 409–417.

Finkelhor, D. and Browne, A. (1985) 'The traumatic impact of child sexual abuse: A conceptualization.' *American Journal of Orthopsychiatry 55*(4), 530–541.

Furniss, T. (1991) *The Multi-Professional Handbook of Child Sexual Abuse: Integrated Management, Therapy, and Legal Intervention.* Florence, KY: Taylor and Francis/ Routledge.

Gjermenia, E., Van Hookb, M. P., Gjipali, S., Xhillari, L., Lungue, F. and Hazizif, A. (2008) 'Trafficking of children in Albania: Patterns of recruitment and reintegration.' *Child Abuse and Neglect 32*, 941–48.

Goodman-Brown, T. B., Edelstein, R. S., Goodman, G. S., Jones, D. P. H. and Gordon, D. S. (2003) 'Why children tell: A model of children's disclosure of sexual abuse.' *Child Abuse and Neglect 27*(5), 525–540.

Hartup, W. W. (1999) *Peer Experience and Its Developmental Significance.* New York, NY: Psychology Press.

Hébert, M., Tourigny, M., Cyr, M., McDuff, P. and Joly, J. (2009) 'Prevalence of childhood sexual abuse and timing of disclosure in a representative sample of adults from the province of Quebec.' *Canadian Journal of Psychiatry 54*, 631– 636.

Helgeson, V. S., Reynolds, K. A. and Tomich, P. L. (2006) 'A meta-analytic review of benefit finding and growth.' *Journal of Consulting and Clinical Psychology 74*(5), 797–816.

Hershkowitz, I., Lanes, O. and Lamb, M. E. (2007) 'Exploring the disclosure of child sexual abuse with alleged victims and their parents.' *Child Abuse and Neglect 31*(2), 111–123.

HM Government (2013) *Working together to safeguard children: A guide to inter-agency working to safeguard and promote the welfare of children.* London: Department for Education, DFE-00300-2013.

Humphrey, J. A. and White, J. W. (2000) 'Women's vulnerability to sexual assault from adolescence to young adulthood.' *Journal of Adolescent Health 27*(6), 419– 424.

Hunter, S. V. (2011) 'Disclosure of child sexual abuse as a life-long process: Implications for health professionals.' *Australian and New Zealand Journal of Family Therapy 32*, 159–172.

Jackson, S., Newall, E., and Backett-Milburn, K. (2015) 'Children's narratives of sexual abuse.' *Child and Family Social Work 20*(3), 322–332.

Jensen, T. K., Gulbrandsen, W., Mossige, S., Reichelt, S. and Tjersland, O. A. (2005) 'Reporting possible sexual abuse: A qualitative study on children's perspectives and the context for disclosure.' *Child Abuse and Neglect 29*(12), 1395–1413.

Jones, D. (2000) 'Editorial: Disclosure of child sexual abuse.' *Child Abuse and Neglect 24*, 269–271.

Jonzon, E. and Lindblad, F. (2004) 'Disclosure, reactions, and social support: Findings from a sample of adult victims of child sexual abuse.' *Child Maltreatment 9*(2), 190–200.

Kellogg, N. D. and Huston, R. L. (1995) 'Unwanted sexual experiences in adolescents: Patterns of disclosure.' *Clinical Pediatrics 34*(6), 306–312.

Kogan, S. M. (2004) 'Disclosing unwanted sexual experiences: Results from a national sample of adolescent women.' *Child Abuse and Neglect 28*(2), 147–165.

Ladd, G. W. (2005) *Children's Peer Relations and Social Competence: A Century of Progress*. New Haven, CT: Yale University Press.

Lalor, K. (ed.) (2001) *The End of Innocence: Child Sexual Abuse in Ireland*. Dublin: Oak Tree Press. Available at http://arrow.dit.ie/aaschsslbk, accessed on 3 March 2016.

Lalor, K. and McElvaney, R. (2010) 'Child sexual abuse, links to later sexual exploitation/high-risk sexual behavior, and prevention/treatment programs.' *Trauma, Violence, and Abuse 11*(4), 159–177.

Lamb, M., Hershkowitz, I., Orbach, Y. and Esplin, P. (2008) *Tell Me What Happened: Structured Investigative Interviews of Children and Witnesses*. Chichester: John Wiley Sons.

Lampe, A. (2002) 'Prävalenz von sexuellem Mißbrauch, physischer Mißhandlung und emotionaler Vernachlässigung in Europa.' *Zeitschrift für Psychosomatische Medizin und Psychotherapie 48*, 4, 370–380. ['Prevalence of sexual abuse and emotional neglect in Europe.' *Journal of Psychosomatic Medicine and Psychotherapy 48*(4), 370–380.]

La Greca, A. and Harrison, H. (2005) 'Adolescent peer relations, friendships, and romantic relationships: Do they predict social anxiety and depression?' *Journal of Clinical Child and Adolescent Psychology 34*(1), 49–61.

Lev-Wiesel, R., Amir, M. and Besser, A. (2005). 'Posttraumatic growth among female survivors of childhood sexual abuse in relation to the perpetrator identity.' *Journal of Loss and Trauma 10*(1), 7–17.

Linley, P. A. and Joseph, S. (2004) 'Positive change following trauma and adversity: A review.' *Journal of Traumatic Stress 17*(1), 11–21.

Livingstone, S., Haddon, L., Gorzig, A. and Olafsson, K. (2011) *EU Kids Online: final report 2011*. London: LSE Library Services/Research Online.

London, K., Bruck, M., Ceci, S. J. and Shuman, D. W. (2007) 'Disclosure of Child Sexual Abuse: A Review of the Contemporary Empirical Literature.' In M. E. Pipe, M. E. Lamb, Y. Orbach and A. C. Cederborg (eds) *Child Sexual Abuse: Disclosure, Delay and Denial*. Mahwah, NJ: Lawrence Erlbaum Associates.

Lovett, B. B. (2004) 'Child sexual abuse disclosure: Maternal response and other variables impacting the victim.' *Child and Adolescent Social Work Journal 21*(4), 355–371.

Lyon, T. D. (2007) 'False Denials: Overcoming Methodological Biases in Abuse Disclosure Research.' In M. Pipe, M. Lamb, Y. Orbach and A. C. Cederborg (eds) *Child Sexual Abuse: Disclosure, Delay and Denial*. Mahweh, NJ: Lawrence Erlbaum Associates.

Lyon, T. D., and Dente, J. A. (2012) 'Child witnesses and the Confrontation Clause.' *Journal of Criminal Law and Criminology 102*, 1181–1232.

Malloy, L. C., Lyon, T. D. and Quas, J. A. (2007) 'Filial dependency and recantation of child sexual abuse allegations.' *Journal of the American Academy of Child and Adolescent Psychiatry 46*(2), 162–170.

Mayock, P., Kitching, K. and Morgan, M. (2007) *RSE in the context of SPHE: An assessment of the challenges to full implementation of the programme in postprimary schools.* Dublin: Crisis Pregnancy Agency/Department of Education and Science.

McCann, I. L. and Pearman, L. A. (1990) *Psychological Trauma and the Adult Survivor.* New York, NY: Brunner-Routledge.

McElvaney, R. (2002) 'Delays in Reporting Childhood Sexual Abuse and Implications for Legal Proceedings.' In D. P. Farrington, C. R. Hollin and M. McMurran (eds) *Sex and Violence: The Psychology of Crime and Risk Assessment.* London, UK: Routledge.

McElvaney, R. (2008) *Containing the secret of child sexual abuse.* Unpublished dissertation. Trinity College, Dublin.

McElvaney, R. (2015a) 'Disclosure of child sexual abuse: Delays, non-disclosure and partial disclosure; what the research tells us and implications for practice.' *Child Abuse Review 24*(3), 159–169.

McElvaney, R. (2015b) *How Children Tell: Containing the Secret of Child Sexual Abuse.* Saarbrucken: Lambert Academic Publishing.

McElvaney, R., and Culhane, M. (2015) 'A retrospective analysis of children's assessment reports: What helps children tell? *Child Abuse Review*, doi: 10.1002/car.2390

McElvaney, R., Greene, S. and Hogan, D. (2012) 'Containing the secret of child sexual abuse.' *Journal of Interpersonal Violence 27*(6), 1155–1175.

McElvaney, R., Greene, S. and Hogan, D. (2014) 'To tell or not to tell? Factors influencing young people's informal disclosures of child sexual abuse.' *Journal of Interpersonal Violence 29*(5), 928–947.

McElvaney, R. and Lalor, K. (2014) 'Child Abuse in Europe.' In J. Conte (ed.) *Child Abuse and Neglect Worldwide.* Washington, DC: Praeger Publishers.

McGee, H., Garavan, R., deBarra, M., Byrne, J. and Conroy, R. (2002) *The SAVI Report: Sexual Abuse and Violence in Ireland.* Dublin: The Liffey Press.

Melrose, M. and Pearce, J. (eds) (2013) *Critical Perspectives on Child Sexual Exploitation and Sexual Trafficking.* London: Palgrave Macmillan.

Medierådet (The Swedish Media Council) (2010) *Ungar och medier 2010. Fakta om barns och ungas användning och upplevelser av medier. [Young persons and media 2008. Facts about childrens' and young person's use and experience of media].* Stockholm: The Swedish Media Council.

Mudaly, N. and Goddard, C. (2006) *The Truth is Longer Than a Lie: Children's Experiences of Abuse and Professional Interventions.* London: Jessica Kingsley.

O'Leary, P. J., Coohey, C. and Easton, S. D. (2010) 'The effect of severe child sexual abuse and disclosure on mental health during adulthood.' *Journal of Child Sexual Abuse 19*, 275–289.

Paine, M. L. and Hansen, D. J. (2002) 'Factors influencing children to self-disclose sexual abuse.' *Clinical Psychology Review 22*, 271–295.

Pearlman, L. and Saakvitne, K. (1995) *Trauma and the Therapist: Countertransference and Vicarious Traumatization in Psychotherapy with Incest Survivors.* New York, NY: Norton.

Pereda, N., Guilera, G., Forns, M. and Gómez-Benito, J. (2009) 'The international epidemiology of child sexual abuse: A continuation of Finkelhor (1994).' *Child Abuse and Neglect 33*, 331–342.

Priebe, G. and Svedin, C. G. (2008) 'Child sexual abuse is largely hidden from the adult society: An epidemiological study of adolescents' disclosures.' *Child Abuse and Neglect 32*(12), 1095–1108.

Quayle E, Jonsson L. and Lööf L. (2012) *Online behaviour related to child sexual abuse. Interviews with affected young people.* ROBERT, Risktaking online behaviour, empowerment through research and training. European Union & Council of the Baltic Sea States. Available at http://childcentre.info/robert, accessed on 24 March 2016.

Radford, L., Corral, C., Bradley, C., Fisher, H. *et al.* (2011) *Child Abuse and Neglect in the UK Today.* London: National Society for the Prevention of Cruelty to Children.

Rogers, A. G. (2006) *The Unsayable: The Hidden Language of Trauma.* New York, NY: Random House.

Rosenthal, S., Feiring, C. and Taska, L. (2003) 'Emotional support and adjustment over a year's time following sexual abuse discovery.' *Child Abuse and Neglect 27*(6), 641–661.

Russell, D.E.H. (1986) *The Secret Trauma: Incest in the Lives of Girls and Women.* New York, NY: Basic Books.

Salter, A. C. (1995) *Transforming Trauma: A Guide to Understanding and Treating Adult Survivors of Child Sexual Abuse.* Thousand Oaks, CA, US: Sage Publications, Inc.

Sanders, J., Munford, R., Liebenberg, L. and Ungar, M. (2014) 'Peer paradox: The tensions that peer relationships raise for vulnerable youth.' *Child and Family Social Work*, doi: 10.1111/cfs.12188

Saywitz, K. J., Esplin, P. and Romanoff, S. L. (2007) 'A Holistic Approach to Interviewing and Treating Children in the Legal System.' In M. E. Pipe, M. E. Lamb, Y. Orbach and A. C. Cederborg (eds) *Child Sexual Abuse: Disclosure, Delay and Denial.* Mahwah, NJ: Lawrence Erlbaum Associates.

Schaeffer, P., Leventhal, J. M., and Asnes, A. G. (2011) 'Children's disclosures of sexual abuse: Learning from direct inquiry.' *Child Abuse and Neglect 35*(5), 343–352.

Schönbucher, V., Maier, T., Mohler-Kuo, M., Schnyder, U. and Landolt, M. A. (2012) 'Disclosure of child sexual abuse by adolescents: A qualitative in-depth study.' *Journal of Interpersonal Violence 27*(17), 3486–3513.

Sgroi, S., Blick, L. and Porter, F. A. (1982) 'A Conceptual Framework for Child Sexual Abuse.' In S. Sgroi (ed.) *Handbook of Clinical Intervention in Child Sexual Abuse.* Lexington, MA: Lexington Books.

Silbert, M. H. (1982) 'Victimization of street prostitutes.' *Victimology 7*, 1–4.

Sirles, E. A. and Frank, P. J. (1989) 'Factors influencing mothers' reactions to intrafamily sexual abuse.' *Child Abuse and Neglect 13*, 131–139.

Sjöberg, R. L. and Lindblad, F. (2002) 'Limited disclosure of sexual abuse in children whose experiences were documented by videotape.' *The American Journal of Psychiatry 159*, 312–314.

Slonim-Nevo, V. and Mukaka, L. (2007) Child abuse and AIDS related knowledge, attitudes and behaviour among adolescents in Zambia. *Child Abuse and Neglect 31*, 143–159.

Smith, D. W., Letourneau, E. J., Saunders, B. E., Kilpatrick, D. G., Resnick, H. S. and Best, C. L. (2000) 'Delay in disclosure of childhood rape: Results from a national survey.' *Child Abuse and Neglect 24*, 273–287.

Sperry, D. M., and Gilbert, B. O. (2005) 'Child peer sexual abuse: Preliminary data on outcomes and disclosure experiences.' *Child Abuse and Neglect 29*(8), 889–904.

Staller, K. M. and Nelson-Gardell, D. (2005) '"A burden in your heart": Lessons of disclosure from female preadolescent and adolescent survivors of sexual abuse.' *Child Abuse and Neglect 29*(12), 1415–1432.

Stoltenborgh, M., van IJzendoorn, M. H., Euser, E. M. and Bakermans-Kranenburg, M. (2011) 'A global perspective on child sexual abuse: Meta-analysis of prevalence around the world.' *Child Maltreatment, 16*(2), 79–101.

Summit, R. C. (1983) 'The child sexual abuse accommodation syndrome.' *Child Abuse and Neglect 7*(2), 177–193.

Tedeschi, R. G. and Calhoun, L. G. (2004) 'Target article: 'posttraumatic growth: Conceptual foundations and empirical evidence.' *Psychological Inquiry 15*(1), 1–18.

Tucker, S. (2011) 'Listening and believing: An examination of young people's perceptions of why they are not believed by professionals when they report abuse and neglect.' *Children and Society 25*, 458–469.

Ullman, S. E. (2007) 'Relationship to perpetrator, disclosure, social reactions, and PTSD symptoms in child sexual abuse survivors.' *Journal of Child Sexual Abuse 16*(1), 19–36.

Ungar, M., Barter, K., McConnell, S. M., Tutty, L. M. and Fairholm, J. (2009a) 'Patterns of abuse disclosure among youth.' *Qualitative Social Work 8*, 341–356.

Ungar, M., Tutty, L. M., McConnell, S., Barter, K. and Fairholm, J. (2009b) 'What Canadian youth tell us about disclosing abuse.' *Child Abuse and Neglect 33*(10), 699–708.

Ungdomsstyrelsen, I. and The Swedish National Board for Youth Affairs (Ungdomsstyrelsen) (2009) 'Erfarenheter av sexuell exponering och sex mot ersättning.' I Ungdomsstyrelsen 2009:9 (ed.) *Se mig. Unga om sex och Internet* (s. 148–181). Stockholm: Ungdomsstyrelsen. ['Experiences of sexual exposure and sex in exchange for compensation.' In The Swedish National Board for Youth Affairs 2009:9 (edn.) *See Me. Young People on Sex and the Internet* (pp. 148–181).] Stockholm: Ungdomsstyrelsen.

UNICEF (2011) *Child Safety Online: Global challenges and strategies.* Florence, Italy: UNICEF. Available at www.unicef-irc.org/publications/pdf/ict_eng.pdf, accessed on 3 March 2016.

UNICEF (2016) *Female Genital Mutilation/Cutting: A Global Concern.* Available at www.unicef.org/media/files/FGMC_2016_brochure_final_UNICEF_SPREAD.pdf, accessed on 16 April 2016.

Vincent, S. and Daniel, B. (2004) 'An analysis of children and young people's calls to ChildLine about abuse and neglect: A study for the Scottish child protection review.' *Child Abuse Review 13*(2), 158–171.

Waterman, C .K. and Foss-Goodman, D. (1984). 'Child molesting: Variables relating to attribution of fault to victims, offenders and nonparticipating parents.' *Journal of Sex Research 20*(4), 329–349.

Wolak, J., Finkelhor, D. and Mitchell, K. J. (2004) 'Internet-initiated sex crimes against minors: Implications for prevention based on findings from a national study.' *Journal of Adolescent Health 35*, 424.e11-20.

# INDEX